When Peoples Speak
to Peoples

HAROLD E. SNYDER

When Peoples Speak
to Peoples

AN ACTION GUIDE TO
INTERNATIONAL CULTURAL RELATIONS
FOR AMERICAN ORGANIZATIONS, INSTITUTIONS,
AND INDIVIDUALS

AMERICAN COUNCIL ON EDUCATION
WASHINGTON, D.C.

PRINTED IN THE UNITED STATES OF AMERICA BY GEORGE BANTA PUBLISHING CO.
MENASHA, WISCONSIN

Foreword

IN THIS DAY when great social and political forces are awake in all parts of the world, we tend to forget how important the role of the individual person can be. The complexity of international problems obscures at times the moral, social, and humanitarian motives which influence human behavior and ultimately the actions of nations. This book starts from the thesis that the human being is central in foreign affairs. If person-to-person and group-to-group relationships are the basis of all social development, it would seem reasonable that by practicing, expanding, and strengthening such relationships internationally, we increase our ability as a free people to cope with the problems which face us. Such relationships can also serve to cultivate abroad a better understanding of the genius of American democracy.

Based primarily upon the experience of the author since 1944, while serving successively as director of training of the United Nations Relief and Rehabilitation Administration, director of the Commission for International Educational Reconstruction and of the Commission on the Occupied Areas of the American Council on Education, and of the Washington Seminar of the American Friends Service Committee, this volume presents both a record of postwar American endeavor in the field of international cultural relations and a series of suggestions for future voluntary efforts. In the total postwar endeavor in international cultural affairs, literally scores of American agencies and thousands of individuals have played a part, desirably supplementing and complementing the work of governments and of international organizations. These special activities of the author supply background for the "action guide" which should illuminate usefully for all readers the practical possibilities of voluntary international service.

This book should clarify considerably the complex relationships between governmental, intergovernmental, and private endeavors in international cultural relations. In consequence, it should help to bridge the gap between what we know and what we do in world affairs.

ARTHUR S. ADAMS, *President*
American Council on Education

November 6, 1951

Preface

THIS VOLUME has two primary purposes, reflected in its division into two rather distinct parts. The purpose of Part I is to try to throw at least a little new light upon the significance of international cultural relations, with special reference to the development in the United States of voluntary action approaches during and since World War II. The purpose of Part II is to provide a convenient guide or manual for use by American voluntary agencies and educational institutions seeking to develop sound programs of international cultural relations.

The author has received the generous collaboration of scores of agencies and individuals in preparing this volume. While the ideas expressed were derived from many sources, the author takes full responsibility for the selection of materials and for their final form. Since the type of organization of the material in Part II has never before been attempted, occasional errors and omissions have doubtless occurred.

Unfortunately, within the limited scope of this volume, it was not possible to do justice to, or even list, all important agencies and projects concerned with each of the twenty-five approaches to international cultural relations described in Part II. To have done so would have diminished the volume's usefulness as an "action manual." The listing of agencies under the various headings is therefore largely for illustrative purposes and is not intended to be comprehensive.

It was difficult to fit some projects into the twenty-five categories selected for treatment in Part II. For example, international student houses with residence facilities are combined for treatment with "international centers," which include also smaller non-residence centers designed largely for non-students. Obviously, any attempt at classification runs the risk of oversimplification. The author will greatly appreciate having errors and omissions called to his attention. Such corrections will be taken into account in any later edition of the manual.

The author wishes to express particular gratitude to his capable assistants, Jean Sartorius and Johanna van den Berg, who carried much of the load of correspondence and organization of the material, particularly during the period near the conclusion of the project when he was abroad.

The general point of view and form of organization reflect to a considerable degree the thinking and effort of the advisory committee for the project. Members of this committee not only guided the project in its early stages, and lent encouragement to the author, but also read and criticized parts of the manuscript. These are: President Herman B Wells, Indiana University; State Superintendent of Maryland Schools, Thomas G. Pullen, chairman respectively of the Commission on the Occupied Areas and the Commission for International Educational Reconstruction; Professor Karl W. Bigelow, Teachers College, Columbia University; and President A. J. Brumbaugh, Shimer College, University of Chicago, vice-chairman respectively of COA and CIER; Vice-President Livingston L. Blair, American National Red Cross; Executive Secretary William G. Carr of the National Education Association of the United States; and Staff Associate Francis J. Brown, American Council on Education.

Others who contributed counsel and specific information include:

Officials of professional and other voluntary agencies: Frederick Abbuhl; H. B. Allen; Paul B. Anderson; DeWitt C. Baldwin; Alice Ball; Colin Bell; Paul Bernick; Nora Booth; Bernice Bridges; Howard L. Brooks; Sterling W. Brown; Christina M. Buechner; Elizabeth B. Burns; Steward G. Cole; Alden H. Emery; Margaret E. Forsyth; Stephen Galatti; Austin Gaugel; Willard E. Givens; Frederick G. Hochwalt; John W. Hollister; Lewis M. Hoskins; Hugh Jenkins; Joan Kain; Paul H. Kinsel; Wilmer J. Kitchen; Vanett Lawler; Mary E. Leeper; Edna MacDonough; William E. McManus; Frederic G. Melcher; Philip

Mettger; MacEnnis Moore; Maude W. Muller; Margaret O'Donoghue; Margaret Olmsted; Charlotte Owen; Janet Paine; Dexter Perkins; Mrs. Henry P. Russell; Marjorie P. Schauffler; Donald Schaumer; Louis Schneider; Herbert Schueller; Herbert L. Seamans; George Pope Shannon; Carleton Smith; Mary H. Smith; William Snyder; Kathleen P. Sparkman; Robert Stanforth; Charlotte Trego; Robert L. Tesdell; Frances B. Townley; Helen Hiett Waller; Donald B. Watt, Jr.; Allen White; Edward N. Wright; Robert Yeaton.

Officials of governmental and intergovernmental agencies: Margretta S. Austin; Elizabeth Beeson; William D. Carter; Luther Evans; David E. Finley; J. Harold Goldthorpe; Leeds Gulick; Frank N. Orenstein; Helen Dwight Reid; Arthur Ringland; Constance Roach; Paul Smith; John Taylor.

College and school officials and other educators: Arthur S. Adams; Christian O. Arndt; Lawrence L. Bethel; William S. Carlson; Donald Cottrell; W. Rex Crawford; Chris A. DeYoung; Roy Tasco Davis; George W. Diemer; Milton E. Eisenhower; Peter Fraenkel; Mortimer Graves; William H. Lemmel; Clarence E. Linton; Milton E. Muelder; John W. Nason; Howard P. Smith; Seth Spaulding; Philip W. Thayer; Frances Thompson; William P. Tolley; Stanley D. Tylman; Gilbert F. White.

Finally, the author wishes to express his appreciation to the Rockefeller Foundation for providing the financial support for this project and for the wise counsel and helpful assistance supplied from time to time by several of its officers, particularly by Janet E. Paine, assistant secretary of the foundation. The encouragement and understanding of the author's wife, Betty Linton Snyder, and his daughters Anadel and Merida Jane were of inestimable value in all stages of the project.

H. E. S.

Contents

PART I

Cultural Relations
in the Postwar World

1.

International Relations as Human Relations

M**ANY RECENT BOOKS** dealing with international problems and ways of coping with them begin with the shock approach. They vigorously remind us of growing world tension, of vastly increased scientific potentialities for the destruction of civilization. They stress the threat of communism, the horrors which totalitarian rule can bring. They emphasize the ominous time factor, the vital necessity of accelerating the forces which can make for peace. With this prelude they move on to the author's proposals for stemming the tide.

If the author is an educator, the solution is likely to lie in the educational process. If he is a social scientist, peace can be preserved only by extending and applying the knowledge of the historian, the economist, the psychologist, or the anthropologist. If he is a clergyman or a philosopher, nothing short of a change in man's morals, value systems, and religious outlook will suffice. If he is a political leader, a diplomat, or a journalist, political solutions are likely to be stressed, either through international agencies, or by-passing them. If he is a military man, strategic considerations are paramount.

This book is no exception in recognizing the vast importance of many of these approaches. The author sincerely intended, however, to make it a decided exception by assuming them, moving on to his proposals. The intelligent reader, likely to examine a volume on so forbidding and presumably boring a subject as international cultural relations, would surely not need to be reminded of the kind of world he lives in. To expand on this would be a mere repetition of the obvious.

3

Unfortunately for some readers, this introductory chapter was undergoing revision in May 1952, when a story in the daily press caught the author's eye. This news story started a chain of recollections which caused him to compromise with his resolve to abstain from the "build-up." He succumbed to the temptation to recount a vivid personal experience, which seems to him to bear upon the theme of the first chapter. It will be left to the reader to draw implications, if any, for the remainder of the book.

In May 1952 our press carried an account of the success in several major municipal elections in Italy of the combined neofascist-monarchist party, with a brief description of its mass persuasion tactics. This followed, by only a few days, fresh accounts of the rise in Germany of ultranationalist political groups with a strong Nazi flavor. Only a week before stories had appeared of tactics used by so-called "hate groups" in our own country, injecting themselves into the presidential campaign.

The story from Italy had a peculiarly familiar ring. A look at some old clippings established the connection. Exactly twenty years earlier, in May 1932, when the author was an exchange student at the University of Leipzig, he had an experience strangely reminiscent of the news of the day. His experience was not unique. Many such reports have doubtless been given before. But it did seem to have special pertinence to a discussion of the human factor in world affairs. At any rate, here it is!

A MASS MEETING IN HITLER'S GERMANY

The spring and summer of 1932 were a time of death struggle for the tottering Weimar Republic. The growing Nazi movement had chosen this year for its determined bid for power. Election followed upon election. These included the final runoff for the presidency of the German Republic, pitting Adolph Hitler against the incumbent octogenarian, General von Hindenburg.

Late in the campaign, one of the largest of the Nazi mass meetings was scheduled for Leipzig, with Hitler as speaker. Any young American student might have been motivated by curiosity to attend. To a student of the social sciences, steeped in the methodology of political science, psychology, and sociology, this was an opportunity not to be missed. What manner of man was this firebrand who promised so glibly to discard the Treaty of Versailles and lift Germany by its own bootstraps to a position of world leadership and world domination? Impelled perhaps by a combination of curiosity and apprehension, a similar desire to witness the event was expressed by the conservative democratic family of the German professor of archeology, with whom the student lived.

The day after the announcement found them in a long line at local Nazi party headquarters in search of the required tickets. Other political parties were pleased to offer free seats, sometimes even free beer, but those attending Nazi rallies bought tickets for the privilege of being harangued and entertained. The tickets provided another surprise. In large letters ticketholders were warned to claim their seats an hour before the scheduled time of the meeting.

On the appointed evening, four skeptics—three German and one American—grumbling a bit at the prospect of a wasted hour, followed the crowds to the meeting place. This proved to be an improvised auditorium, the largest exhibit hall of the famous Leipzig Trade Fair. Approaching the *Messhalle,* they noticed to their surprise that the crowd divided. Nearly half entered the only slightly smaller adjoining exhibit hall. Inquiry revealed that these were not rival meetings, but were actually the same. So many tickets had been demanded that an additional hall had been hired, with seats sold at the same price and under the same conditions. The unfortunate late purchasers were promised only loudspeaker transmission of *der Führer's* speech, plus a glimpse of him as he marched through their building to the main auditorium.

A few minutes before the seven o'clock deadline for claiming seat reservations, more than three hours before Hitler's scheduled arrival, the hall was crowded, save for a block of seats held for party leaders. The atmosphere was already tense and expectant. Smiling, smartly uniformed, braided Hitler-*Mädchen* in their late teens, sporting the swastika, showed ticketholders to their seats to the accompaniment of traditional folksongs played by a large brass band on the stage.

Once seated, there was general haste to begin the typical German supper of *Bratwurst,* cheese, and black bread, standard fare even between the acts of the opera. The whole audience, numbering nearly 10,000, was content to divide its attention between eating, listening to the popular, traditional, and patriotic airs, and observing with admiration the husky young storm troopers marching arrogantly up and down the main aisle, or standing motionless with folded arms along the walls.

When attention lagged, flamboyant party literature could be purchased from attractive, uniformed girls. Or the slogans on huge signs on the walls could be read and discussed with one's neighbors. That these slogans merely repeated the blatant headlines of the Nazi press made little difference in their impact. Even the trite ambiguity of "Germany Awake," "Avenge the Injustice of Versailles," "Abolish Unemployment," and "Germany Will Lead Again," seemed to many to take on new meaning in this setting. Only the harsh cruelty of a sign reading "Down with the Jews" struck a highly divisive note, serving as a reminder of one fundamental difference between the National Socialists and the political parties of the left and center. At smaller political rallies, aimed at the working classes and at students, the American had heard other slogans, tailor-made for the audience. To the workers Hitlerism had been portrayed as the only true means to achieving a fully socialized state. To the students and middle classes, it had been depicted as the last bulwark of capitalism. But even at these special meetings Nazi racism and the preoccupation with the scapegoat never varied. Before this large, diverse audience, even the Communists incurred less venom than did the Jews.

Promptly at eight the meeting began. First an announcement. The audience was told that in his heroic effort to save the German people, Hitler refused to spare himself. So to bring his message to the greatest possible number of people during the latter days of the campaign, he had to speak in several cities during the same evening. The elderly announcer then informed the audience of Hitler's arrival in Dresden, 75 miles away, for the first of three addresses scheduled that evening. In emotion-choked tones, the speaker described Hitler's reception in Dresden, the many dignitaries who had greeted him at the airport, the flowers and other tributes lavished upon him. The audience was alerted for a later report on Hitler's message to the people of Dresden.

The regular program of the evening began when a young man in working-class garb strode to the platform, introduced himself, told where he lived, and named the factory where he worked. Then in simple language, but in familiar slogans, he told in ten minutes why he was for Hitler. He was followed by a girl university student, then by a farmer, a housewife, a clerk, an unemployed teacher, a minor government employee, a doctor, members of the *Hitlerjugend* of both sexes, a war veteran minus a leg. More than a dozen speakers in all, representing virtually every segment of German life, told their story. Each was brief and spoke with a practiced sincerity. All described the awful living conditions and insecurity afflicting those in their station of life. All offered virtually identical reasons why persons of their background would vote for Hitler. None offered even the rudiments of a positive program. All stressed implicit faith in The Man: "He will find a way to lead us."

The logic was negative. What have we to lose? Have not all other methods failed? Did not monarchy bring defeat in World War I? Did not the Socialist regime which followed bring civil strife and ruinous inflation? Was not the current conservative democracy bringing unemployment and misery? Had not America and Britain become rich and prosperous at Germany's expense? Had not Mussolini brought order in Italy out of similar chaos? Had not Bismarck, Frederick the Great, and the old Teutons employed authoritarian methods to fill the most glorious pages of German history? Was not any change now better than the present insecurity? What had Germans to lose but their hunger and their chains?

Evident throughout were pathological self-pity, desire to place the blame anywhere but upon themselves, preoccupation with Germany's manifest destiny, and contemptuous disregard for logic, reason, and cooperation as avenues to progress. "The trouble with Germans is that they have never learned to hate" was heard repeatedly.

But to the American, studying that year with the famous psychologist Edward Spranger, and with the Leipzig disciples of Wilhelm Wundt, the most interesting aspect of the meeting was the careful preparation for the arrival of *der Führer*. After the fourth speaker, the emotional announcer, now unseen, reported over the amplifiers on Hitler's address in Dresden—the size of the audience, how additional thousands, unable to get into the hall, stood in the rain outside the building. A few excerpts from Hitler's talk, the length and obvious enthusiasm of his ovation were reported. The tension of the Leipzig audience heightened perceptibly as the announcement closed with the report that Hitler was at that very moment at the Dresden airport, about to depart on the short flight to Chemnitz, for his second talk of the evening.

A half-hour later, another interruption! Hitler had arrived in Chemnitz. A bit later a description of this meeting and word of his departure for Leipzig. The latter announcement produced a prolonged burst of hysterical applause and cheering. With each report the audience had grown more and more expectant. The atmosphere became electric when, suddenly, right in the middle of a speech, the unseen announcer interrupted: "Ladies and gentlemen." Several seconds of carefully calculated silence, protected by ten thousand bated breaths. A cough or sneeze would have been sacrilege. The announcement resumed. Hitler was now actually at the Leipzig airport. Party dignitaries were there to receive him. In another twenty minutes, an event of lifelong significance to all would occur. They would actually be in the presence of the demigod. The announcer's emotion had grown conveying the significance of the occasion. Yet each word was deliberately pronounced in a studied effort to avoid unintelligibility. After the announcement, another second of silence, then the delayed reaction. The audience seemed to rise spontaneously. Pandemonium broke loose. Cheering, singing, hugging, back slapping in a demonstration for the as-yet-absent Hitler lasted several minutes. When the crowd finally quieted down, the speaking continued, but now no one listened. Each was steeling himself for the great moment to come.

Abruptly, as a distinguished, elderly *Gymnasium* teacher was speaking, the hall was plunged into darkness. A searchlight, hitherto hidden by the draperies, beamed from the ceiling above the stage toward the rear entrance. Two bands joined in the playing of the "Horst Wessel Lied"; the audience leapt to its feet and gasped. The tallest and handsomest stormtroopers marched down the center aisle and formed an honor guard on either side. A score of party officials followed, and finally *der Führer* himself.

To the cynical American, this was indeed the denouement, the mountain laboring to bring forth a mouse. Could this indeed be the modern counterpart of Frederick the Great, almost of the Nordic gods? Short, dark, presenting a comical appearance with his Charlie Chaplin mustache, he strutted with outstretched right arm, with a ludicrous swagger reminiscent of Mussolini. Surely the audience would be disillusioned, would now see how ridiculous the whole build-up had been. On the contrary, as soon as it had caught its collective breath, the shouts, the backslapping, the hugging, and the singing dwarfed the earlier demonstration. Even the two brass bands were drowned out. It was as if the most eloquent inspirational oration had already been delivered. While receiving the plaudits of the crowd, Hitler stood soberly on the platform, right arm still outstretched. Finally, with an impatient gesture, he indicated his readiness to speak.

In hoarse, screaming tones he shouted for twenty minutes the same slogans, generalities, and clichés already mouthed many times by previous speakers. Nothing of significance was added, either in content or in delivery. His accent and inflection, those of the Bavarian or Austrian peasant, would normally have been found distasteful or ludicrous to the many cultured Germans in the audience.

But, to the relatively disinterested listener, the response was unbelievable. The termination of the talk was the signal for a wild demonstration, lasting fully twenty minutes, in which every individual present seemed to be playing an active part. To the complete astonishment of the American student, even the elderly professor and his conservative wife and daughter were swept up in the emotion, joining in the singing, shouting, and applauding until their hands ached.

After a few days the spell of this emotional experience upon the professor and his family wore off, with one exception. The son, a medical student, who had sat with his comrades in another part of the audience, enrolled almost immediately in the Nazi party. According to a report received recently, he perished in an air raid, after several years of service with the German Army.

The above personal experience is presented with great diffidence, first, because it offers little not recounted many times before; second, because such isolated incidents are susceptible of too-easy generalization; third, because it deals with an abuse of skills derived from the social sciences, while this chapter is designed to emphasize their constructive uses; and finally, because it may seem at first glance to have little to do with the principal purpose of the volume—that of offering guidelines for voluntary action in international cultural relations.

Sometimes, however, important lessons can be learned even from perversions of good ideas. If the Nazi and Communist dictators can employ knowledge of human relations for ulterior ends, must we not accelerate study of its constructive uses?

What Are International Relations?

The remainder of this chapter is largely devoted to citing some of the constructive uses of the "human relations approach." The growing science of human relations can be a powerful weapon to eradicate the social ills which have plagued man since the dawn of history. In developing this weapon, the free world has every advantage. Freedom to study social institutions and the assumptions behind them directly, and even to experiment with them, is scarcely conceivable under totalitarian systems. Without such freedom, ability to arrive at sound conclusions and practicable applications is seriously inhibited.

The basic idea behind the conception of international relations as human relations is startlingly simple. It is the premise that international relations mean relationships between people of varying nationalities. One is almost ashamed to repeat a statement so obvious and trite. In the tradition of intellectual respectability, a basic truth such as this cannot be stated so directly. It must be hidden under a thicket of verbiage, must be couched in linguistic trappings familiar only to specialists in the particular field. Even defining international relations as a "complex congeries of interstate relationships, and of interpersonal and intergroup relations across national boundaries" would be oversimplification to some.

Whatever the definition of international relations, the human factor in the conduct of world affairs cannot longer be denied. It can be, however, and too often is, ignored. Ironically, the human relations aspect of international relations seems to be better recognized by aggressively minded dictators, seeking ways of gaining control over others by subversion and propaganda, than by democratic political leaders. Ideological tags appealing to the normal aspirations and values of the common man facilitate totalitarian penetration. The rapid growth of communism in Asia and other parts of the world cannot be accounted for merely in the traditional terms of diplomacy, economic pressures, or the threat of military force. It is based upon close study and exploitation of the aspirations and fears of the common man.

Yet it remains customary to speak, in the United States and throughout the Western world, of international relations primarily in terms of official relations between states, of purely political factors, of treaties, of formal agreements and declarations, of balance of power, of force and counterforce, with, of course, also some attention to economic factors.

A recent large conference dealing with UNESCO offered as a whole an encouraging demonstration of concern for cultural elements in world affairs. Yet, when the study of international relations as a field of specialization and as a part of general education came under discussion by a study group of university professors of the subject, it was evident they still thought largely in the traditional terms of historical, geographical, and political factors. Little evidence was provided that college courses in international relations have anything to do with the values which peoples of other nations hold; with attitudes, images, and stereotypes held by peoples of one nation toward another; with cultural patterns and trends; with knowledge about how individuals and groups interact; and with the arts of international communication; with the underlying social, religious, ethical, and psychological factors in which political action is rooted.

Signs of Progress

Despite this continuing neglect of the human element in international relations, signs of real progress are on the horizon. The postwar years have witnessed a vast growth in the attention given to the emerging science of human relations, and to its component fields in the social sciences and the humanities. From several different directions, long-dormant forces have begun to converge. These new signs include:

Within government:

1. Accelerated search for ways of supplementing traditional approaches to the conduct of world affairs, based largely upon recognized deficiencies in our handling of relations with other countries during and since the war.

2. New efforts to utilize more fully the contributions of the social sciences and related disciplines, particularly social psychology, anthropology, pedagogy, mass communications, opinion and propaganda analysis, and also psychiatry, and the studies of group relations.

3. Stimulation of social science research, both within the various governmental agencies and under contract with private institutions and organizations.

4. Expansion of educational and cultural relations programs supported with government funds, such as the Fulbright, Smith-Mundt, and leadership exchange programs, and those involved in Point Four and other economic development projects.

5. Increased recognition of the basic importance of the conflict

of ideas, still thought of primarily, however, in terms of information and propaganda.

6. Vastly increased recognition, beginning early in the war and now assuming more permanent status, of the role of sound voluntary effort in achieving results beyond the reach of government, resulting in growing willingness to enter into joint cooperative projects with nongovernmental groups.

Within academic circles:

1. Growing awareness of the international responsibilities of American education and the various disciplines comprising it, applying particularly to the social sciences, but also touching the humanities and natural sciences.

2. Vast expansion of research and teaching aimed at solution of specific international problems with which government is concerned.

3. Increased attention by the various philanthropic foundations to encouragement of study and research relating to problems of war and peace, and to studies of human relations factors in international as well as domestic affairs.

4. New interest in interdisciplinary studies and research.

5. Greater emphasis upon "international understanding" as an objective of general education.

6. Growing recognition of the importance of experiential education stressing direct student participation in practical projects to supplement formal courses.

7. Vastly increased contact since the war between American students, professors, and researchers, and those of other countries.

Within voluntary organizations:

1. On the part of professional, educational, civic, and service organizations, increased emphasis since the war upon direct action in contrast to mere verbal approaches to international relations.

2. A new concept of the role of agencies hitherto wholly domestic in scope, with growing recognition of the importance of developing international relationships.

3. On the part of relief agencies with overseas programs, a reshaping of programs away from exclusive emphasis upon physical relief and toward long-term cultural relations.

4. Greater willingness to develop objective evaluation and research programs aimed at finding and utilizing the best available tools of the social sciences in appraising results.

5. Greater acceptance of voluntary coordinating efforts of recognized professional bodies, aimed at preventing unnecessary duplication and raising standards.

6. Increased readiness to cooperate in joint projects with government and with agencies abroad.

Increasingly, the emphasis upon good human relations as the basis of international relations has brought together all three elements—government, the academic disciplines, and voluntary agencies—in a combined attack upon specific problems. One modest experimental effort, among many, along this line is the Washington Seminar, sponsored by the American Friends Service Committee. Taking as its theme "The Impact of the United States upon Other Peoples," the seminar has brought a group of leading government officials concerned with international programs and policies into contact with persons conducting significant new research in the growing science of human relations. Meetings are kept small, off the record, and informal, with no attempt made to reach specific conclusions. Each person contributes to, and derives from, the discussion whatever may be pertinent to his own field of interest. However, each tries to take a fresh look at his specific daily tasks in the light of new insights deriving from the social sciences and humanities. In an unhurried atmosphere, temporarily freed from the daily pressures for administrative decision, it has been possible to examine assumptions behind both governmental and voluntary programs and to explore the most promising new approaches to the conduct of international affairs.

The seminar has dealt with such topics as the images and stereotypes of the United States held by other peoples, aspirations of youth in different cultures, the implications for international affairs of research in group relations, the individual American abroad as viewed by himself and by others, promising new approaches to selection and preparation of personnel for overseas service, and national values and objectives as factors in international action.

Several other significant interdisciplinary efforts are under way, utilizing similar informal techniques. Some of these are at major universities, others sponsored by such organizations as the Society for the Psychological Study of Social Issues, the Public Administration Clearing House, Arden House near New York, and the Social Science Research Council. Efforts along the same line are being made by the U.S. National Commission for UNESCO, as well as by the parent agency with headquarters in Paris. Abroad, similar attempts are being made under the leadership of such agencies as Tavistock Institute in London and the World Federation for Mental Health.

UNESCO's Influence

In humanizing the concept of international relations, the influence and potentialities of UNESCO are significant. Various aspects of UNESCO's activity are dealt with in the chapters which follow. The keynote to UNESCO's effort in this area is in the preamble to the UNESCO Constitution, which suggests that the origin of wars is to be found in the minds of man, rather than in the formal acts of sovereign states; that war is the product of human misunderstandings; and that peace can result only from "peoples speaking to peoples."

This relatively simple idea has been analyzed and given specific meaning by one of the leading American authorities in international relations, Professor Frederick S. Dunn of Princeton University, in his book *War and the Minds of Men*,[1] published by the Council on Foreign Relations. Professor Dunn emphasizes the vast importance of the work being done in the field of human relations and its potential effect upon the conduct of interstate re-

[1] See bibliography for publication data about the books mentioned in the following paragraphs.

lations. He outlines certain specific steps which UNESCO can take to make its work more effective.

Among UNESCO's most promising projects, utilizing materials from the fields of human relations, is its study of international tensions. This study, headed successively by Hadley C. Cantril, Otto Klineberg, Robert C. Angell, and E. Franklin Frazier, has already produced a number of significant reports, including a symposium in book form, *Tensions That Cause Wars,* edited by Cantril. Another notable study in this field, stemming from UNESCO's work, is Klineberg's *Tensions Affecting International Understanding: A Survey of Research.* This important work summarizes a vast quantity of significant research. The potentialities and limitations of the scientific study of human relations, with special reference to international affairs, are presented under the headings "Personality in Relation to Nationality," "National Stereotypes," "Attitudes and Their Modification," and "Influences Making for Aggression." Among the most interesting parts of the study is a discussion of the conditions under which attitudes may be changed.[2] The *International Social Science Bulletin,* published by UNESCO, also devoted its autumn 1951 issue to "National Stereotypes and International Understanding."

OTHER RECENT STUDIES

Another valuable contribution to the subject of tensions is the volume edited by George W. Kisker, *World Tensions: The Psychopathology of International Relations,* a symposium by twenty-two leading psychologists and psychiatrists of twenty nations. On the subject of stereotypes, *Psychological Factors of Peace and War,* edited by T. H. Pear, draws principally upon European sources.

In the broader field of cultural relations, a recent symposium, *Cultural Groups and Human Relations,* edited by Karl W. Bigelow, consists of lectures delivered before the Conference on Educational Problems of Special Cultural Groups held at Teachers College, Columbia University, during the summer of 1949. This

[2] O. Klineberg, *Tensions Affecting International Understanding: A Survey of Research* (New York: Social Science Research Council, 1950), pp. 138–66.

volume begins with a paper on "Basic Principles in Improving Human Relations," by Gordon W. Allport, an outstanding "frontier thinker" and researcher in human relations. Another paper, by Alvin Zander, on "The Group Process and Human Relations," outlines the contribution of group dynamics to international human relations.

One of the real pioneers in relating human relations research to government administration, in general, and to international programs in particular, is the anthropologist-psychiatrist Alexander H. Leighton. His study during the war of the administration of Japanese relocation centers in the Southwest formed the basis of his book, *The Governing of Men*. Here he derived from an intensive study of the relocation center in Poston, Arizona, a series of principles and recommendations applicable to individuals under stress, with attention to factors involved in their traditional systems of belief and social organization. He concludes with suggestions for administrators, including specific possibilities of using applied social science in government programs, particularly those involving relations with other peoples and cultures. Leighton develops this theme considerably further in a second study, based upon his experience as chief of the Foreign Morale Analysis Division in Japan, studying factors affecting the Japanese morale. This study, *Human Relations in a Changing World: Observations on the Use of the Social Sciences,* amplifies considerably his earlier suggestions for the use of applied social science in relation to government administration in international affairs.

One of the most important contributions to public understanding of the science of human relations is Stuart Chase's *Roads to Agreement: Successful Methods in the Science of Human Relations.* Chase's method is to describe vividly specific action approaches to the problem of how people can learn to get along together. The approaches described cover a wide range, including descriptions of research projects in academic institutions, experiments in group dynamics, examples of labor-management relations in industry, international conferences, and Quaker meetings.

The volumes cited above are merely examples of the growing literature on human relations having a direct bearing upon the conduct of foreign affairs. It is safe to predict that the quantity of such literature will vastly increase during the 1950's, for all workers in the field agree that the surface has hardly been scratched. Significant new studies are already under way. For example, the Department of Social Relations at Harvard University is completing, under Gordon W. Allport's direction, a study of aspirations of youth in ten countries. John Useem, a leading anthropologist, is completing, under the title "Americans as Governors in the Pacific," an analysis of our experience in the former Japanese-mandated islands since the war, including a study of how Americans feel and act in a cross-cultural situation in which they are in a position of authority and leadership. Rensis Likert and his Institute for Social Research of the University of Michigan are in the midst of an important series of studies in this field. The Social Science Research Council, the Institute for Associated Research at Hanover, New Hampshire, the Russian Research Center of Harvard University, the American Anthropological Society, the American Psychological Association, and various departments of Columbia University, the University of Chicago, Cornell University, and Stanford University are conducting or otherwise encouraging new research in cultural and human relations aspects of world affairs. These are only a few of the agencies plowing new ground which may produce in the next decade drastic changes in our concept of international relations.

Values and Human Relations

A leading expert in international affairs, Father Edmund A. Walsh, for a long time head of Georgetown University's School of Foreign Service, which has trained thousands of future American diplomats recently, points out another gap in the conduct of our foreign affairs. He says that too often the United States exhibits "genius for the practical and concrete phenomena of life, coupled with a kind of tone-deafness toward the role of the abstract and metaphysical in the unfolding of world history."[3] Such criticism is frequently voiced abroad, even by our best friends.

[3] E. A. Walsh, *Total Empire* (Milwaukee: Bruce Publishing Co., 1951), p. 27.

The Hitler meeting described at the beginning of the chapter demonstrates how knowledge derived from the social sciences can boomerang, can be employed for ulterior ends. In unscrupulous hands, such skills as those designed to effect attitude changes and to influence human behavior are powerful weapons. Even when the intent is clearly altruistic, the scientific method applied to the study of social institutions and interpersonal relationships is apt to be cold and mechanistic.

The ends to which knowledge deriving from research in human relations is to be put is obviously of first importance. This raises the question of the values we hope to achieve in foreign affairs. Consideration of the value systems underlying man's behavior leads directly into the realm of moral and spiritual forces, of ethics, philosophy, and religion.

The very term "human relations" is broader than the usual scope of the social sciences, and suggests the "humanities." The humanities, as commonly conceived, include philosophy, religion, and the language disciplines essential to human communication. These fields are obviously involved in the "human relations approach" to international affairs. To the extent that the humanities are gradually overcoming their traditional isolation from the market place of everyday affairs, they may be looked to more and more for guidance and insight in the complex sphere of interpersonal, intergroup, and interstate relations.

The struggle for men's minds, sometimes called the war of ideas, is not primarily a conflict of techniques, important as these are. Techniques are meaningless in the absence of clear understanding of the ends they are to serve. Ideological differences are rooted in the assumption that one system of values is higher than another. The skills of both the social scientist and the natural scientist merely provide the means of achieving the desired ends and values.

Leighton, in the course of a discussion of the relationship between social sciences and values, offers an interesting formula for preventing the misuse of the scientific method, as applied to social problems. He suggests that "Within an area marked off for scientific investigation, the values of science reign supreme over each

step in the process toward conclusions and in the conclusions themselves. Moral values, when pertinent, dominate scientific values at
three contiguous points: the selection of the problem to be investi-
gated, the limitation of the human and other materials that may
be used, and the determination of what shall be done with the
results."[4]

Discussing the role of values from the point of view of a social
psychologist, Cantril, in *The "Why" of Man's Experience,* particularly the chapters on "The Characteristics of Man" and "The Development of Men's Characteristics," stresses the "value attributes"
which pervade every human experience, and describes how the
capacity to make value judgments develops. He concludes that
the capacity to experience value attributes is inseparably related
to other human capacities. In a later chapter he points out that the
sense of rightness or wrongness of any action can be just as real
an experience as any other perception, and asserts that "Effective
action in new and emerging situations cannot possibly be gov-
erned solely by logical and rational considerations."[5] But he suggests further that "Perhaps through an intellectual grasp of the
process of value judgment so constantly used in everyday life,
the psychologist can at least point to the direction in which an
improvement of man's capacity to make value judgments must be
sought."[6]

These treatments involve a recognition by social scientists of
the need for attention to moral and spiritual factors, but do not by
any means dispose of this question. They merely open up a vast
new series of problems. As applied to international relations, comparative value systems of different peoples offer a wide, largely
uncharted area for interdisciplinary exploration. Promising bits
of research and inquiry are under way. A few of those which have
recently come to the author's attention are mentioned here for

[4] Alexander Leighton, *Human Relations in a Changing World* (New York: E. P.
Dutton and Co., 1949), p. 210.
[5] Hadley Cantril, *The "Why" of Man's Experience* (New York: Macmillan Co.,
1950), p. 169.
[6] *Ibid.,* p. 171.

illustrative purposes. Allport's new study of aspirations of youth in different cultures has already been cited. David McClelland, of Wesleyan University, has been giving attention to the value systems implicit in children's literature in the Soviet Union, and to differing national approaches to a series of moral dilemmas presented to adult education classes in London, New Haven, and Vienna. F. G. Friedmann, of the department of philosophy at the University of Arkansas, in conducting an experiment in self-help in a poverty-stricken community of southern Italy, is stressing the study of comparative value systems. Questions of this type are also engaging such professional societies as the American Council of Learned Societies. Anthropologists are turning attention increasingly to underlying goals and aspirations as reflected in cultural changes. Leighton, for example, urges going far beyond the analysis of *existing* value systems, and studying *changes* taking place in traditional values. Trends may often be more important than the values themselves. To ascertain quickly and accurately changes and trends affecting political policies and relationships, Leighton proposes the establishment throughout critical areas of the world of field "value weather stations."

A recognition of the vital role of human goals and values in the conduct of international affairs is implicit in much of the material in the later chapters. In dealing with *action* approaches to international relations, particularly those in which Americans are involved, it is essential that contrasting national and subnational value systems be constantly borne in mind. This requires a better understanding of *our own* basic values and goals. Americans tend too readily to assume that the objectives they hold are bound to be shared by those with whom they deal abroad. This glib assumption has done untold damage. But it is more comprehensible to others than is the recurring evidence that many of those who represent us abroad have no clear understanding of our own basic values and objectives. The American who treats others as inferiors is untrue to his own democratic and Christian tradition. Only by clarifying our own scheme of values and the specific objectives comprising them, recognizing and endeavoring to appreciate the value systems and social goals of those with whom we work abroad, can we conduct our "international relations as human relations." Is not such clarification also basic to the efficient handling of foreign affairs?

2.

International Cultural Relations

ANOTHER PROBLEM in conception and semantics is posed in the effort to describe specific program implications of the "human relations approach" in world affairs. Obviously all aspects of the conduct of international relations—governmental, intergovernmental, and voluntary—are involved. Increasingly, however, in recent years specific programs have been developed to promote cross-cultural contacts across national boundaries, in which political implications, if present at all, are decidedly secondary to other aims.

WHAT ARE INTERNATIONAL CULTURAL RELATIONS?

It is to such programs that the term "international cultural relations" has usually been applied. This term is far from satisfactory. To some it is pompous; to others it smacks either of artiness or of the terminology of anthropology. Abroad it may still carry the unsavory flavor of the German use of *Kultur* as a political weapon. Perhaps worst of all, according to Archibald MacLeish, it is a "boring" phrase.[1]

Despite its inadequacy, the term international cultural relations has achieved fairly general acceptance in the United States. Its exact meaning is, however, by no means equally generally understood. In *The Cultural Approach*, R. E. McMurry and Muna Lee define the term as follows: "The cultural relations of a people are its efforts towards mutual acquaintance and the mutual understanding that such acquaintance brings."[2] They add that "any

[1] Ruth E. McMurry and Muna Lee, *The Cultural Approach* (Chapel Hill: University of North Carolina Press, 1947), p. v.
[2] *Ibid.*, p. 1.

program of cultural relations is a program of communication. A nation's culture is the sum total of its achievements; its own expression of its own personality; its way of thinking and acting. Its program of cultural relations abroad is its method of making these things known to foreigners."[3]

This definition implies a conscious effort by a people as a whole, acting through its official agencies, to interpret its culture abroad. It implies further the element of mutuality, "For cultural relationship is essentially that of friendship from people to people, from the citizenry of one country to the citizenry of another, through such channels of mutual acquaintance as make friendship rewarding between individual and individual."[4]

The treatment of cultural relations in this interesting volume by McMurry and Lee is limited to government-sponsored bilateral efforts, although multilateral possibilities through UNESCO and other agencies are also referred to. France, Germany, Japan, the U.S.S.R., Great Britain, Latin America, and the United States are each the subject of a chapter recounting the history of official cultural relations programs up to 1947. The point is stressed that programs of national interpretation may either be largely non-political, or may be directed toward clearly political ends. The totalitarian state has resorted to cultural activities to pave the way for domination over other countries. It is asserted that "On the other hand the democracies have used cultural programs to develop free and friendly relationships between their own and other peoples which lead to mutual understanding and respect and to that intangible goodwill which is a recognized asset in all relationships, individual and collective, whether political, economic or cultural."[5]

A slightly earlier study by I. L. Kandel for the American Council on Education deals with *United States Activities in International Cultural Relations.*[6] This volume stresses private volun-

---

[3] *Ibid.,* pp. 2–3.
[4] *Ibid.,* p. 3.
[5] *Ibid.,* p. 8.
[6] I. L. Kandel, *United States Activities in International Cultural Relations* (Washington: American Council on Education, 1945).

tary effort as well as efforts of the United States government, particularly projects concerned with exchanges of persons and with educational relationships with other countries. Kandel describes the work of the Rockefeller Foundation and other philanthropic agencies, and of the various professional associations. He stresses the point that, until quite recently, our own country left to private effort most activities in the field of cultural relations. He also sketches the development prior to 1945 in the teaching of international relations and comparative education in American universities, and includes an interesting survey of foreign opinions of American education.

United States Government Programs

Kandel's opening phrase, amply justified by recent developments, predicts that "the United States is destined to play a far greater part than ever before in the history of the country in international cultural relations."[7] The surveys of the growth of United States government participation in international cultural relations by Kandel, and by McMurry and Lee, make it unnecessary here to do more than review a few of the high lights of our official programs in this field. Since 1938, when the Division of Cultural Relations was first created within the Department of State, government programs have steadily expanded. Stressing initially relations with Latin America, as a result of pioneer work of the Office of the Coordinator of Inter-American Affairs, our government's program has gradually become world-wide in scope. One of the landmarks in this development was the assignment of cultural relations attachés to embassy and legation staffs in Latin America, and such officers have since been assigned to certain other countries.

The cultural relations functions of the State Department were vastly expanded in 1945 through the transfer to the Department of the informational functions of the Office of Inter-American Affairs. To it were also added the remaining functions of the Office of War Information concerning psychological warfare and the interpretation of United States war aims to allied and neutral

[7] *Ibid.,* p. iv.

nations. These new activities became part of a combined Office of International Information and Cultural Affairs, incorporating the former Division of Cultural Relations. The new office was concerned with (1) the promotion abroad of better understanding of United States aims, policies, and institutions; (2) the coordination of policy and action for programs of the United States in the field of international information and cultural affairs; (3) the furtherance of the international exchange of persons, knowledge, and skills, together with responsibility for integrating with over-all United States foreign policy the programs of other federal agencies involving international exchanges.

Several congressional steps of considerable importance for United States participation in international cultural relations took place between 1946 and 1948. When the United States became an official member of the United Nations Educational, Scientific and Cultural Organization on July 30, 1946, the enabling act called for the establishment of a U.S. National Commission for UNESCO composed of representatives both of governmental and private agencies to advise concerning American relations with UNESCO and to implement UNESCO's program within the United States. A UNESCO Relations Staff was established within the Department of State to serve as the secretariat of the Commission. Many of the activities described throughout this volume have been closely related to the work of this Commission, and of UNESCO proper.

One of the greatest landmarks in United States involvement in international cultural relations was enacted in 1947. Public Law No. 584, popularly known as the Fulbright Act, passed the Seventy-ninth Congress after a vigorous campaign by scores of American private agencies, many of them working in cooperation with the Commission for International Educational Reconstruction on postwar cultural rehabilitation abroad. This ingenious act provided for international exchanges of persons, utilizing foreign currencies deriving from sales of United States war-surplus materials to other governments. Such exchanges were later applied primarily to students, teachers, professors, research workers, and specialists in scientific and in a few other fields.

By 1952 twenty-four countries[8] had Fulbright agreements with the United States. The law is administered by the Board of Foreign Scholarships, under the guidance of the Department of State, and with the assistance of specially created educational foundations in each participating country. Under contractual relationships with the Department of State, selections of American participants are made by four agencies—three private, and one governmental. Professors, research scholars, and other specialists are selected by the Committee on International Exchange of Persons of the Conference Board of Associated Research Councils; university and graduate students, by the Institute of International Education; teachers in public elementary and secondary schools are selected by the United States Office of Education; and teachers assigned to private secondary schools in certain countries are appointed by the Inter-American Schools Service of the American Council on Education.[9]

Since only foreign currencies are available, the act has thus far benefited primarily Americans going abroad, but an increasing number of foreigners have also come to the United States under partial Fulbright grants, covering mainly their ocean transport.

A second act of Congress, of vast importance in fostering United States programs of international cultural relations, followed closely upon the first. Public Law No. 402, popularly known as the Smith-Mundt Act, passed the Eightieth Congress in 1948, also with the active support of voluntary educational and social service agencies engaged in international educational reconstruction. The act authorized interchanges between the United States and other countries of students, trainees, teachers, professors, and many kinds of specialized personnel, as well as general exchanges of information, films, books, and publications in education, science, and the arts. It also established a substantial information program which later included the Voice of America, initiated during the war by the Office of War Information. Later appropriations bills made pos-

[8] Australia, Austria, Belgium and Luxembourg, Burma, China (suspended), Denmark, Egypt, France, Greece, India, Iran, Iraq, Italy, Japan, Korea (suspended), Netherlands, New Zealand, Norway, Pakistan, Philippines, Thailand, Turkey, and the United Kingdom.
[9] See Appendix for addresses of agencies mentioned.

sible the implementation of this act which was intended in part to provide United States currency to supplement the foreign currencies available under the Fulbright Act. An important provision of the act was the establishment of official Advisory Commissions on Educational Exchange and Information, with secretariats in the Department of State. This act provides that it shall be the duty of the Secretary of State to utilize, to the maximum extent practicable, the services and facilities of private agencies in administering the program.

Other congressional efforts to promote international cultural relations in one form or another have included (1) provision for educational and cultural programs as an aspect of military government in occupied areas; (2) permission within the GI Bill of Rights (Public Law No. 346, Seventy-eighth Congress) to war veterans to study abroad as well as in the United States; (3) special legislation on behalf of Chinese students stranded in the United States; and (4) educational assistance in appropriations for Korean relief, to mention only a few.

Early in 1952 a new agency was created within the Department of State, technically independent of the office of the Assistant Secretary for Public Affairs, which had directed the Department's varied and growing cultural relations programs. This new agency is the United States International Information Administration, with the former president of Washington State College, Wilson S. Compton, as Administrator. This office combined five service offices, concerned with international broadcasting, international press, international motion pictures, international information centers, and international educational exchanges.

The creation of this new Administration resulted partly from congressional demands for separation of the Voice of America and other information activities from direct State Department supervision. The Smith-Mundt Act's provision for combined information and educational exchange activities under a single direction has from the first been a subject of considerable controversy. Some of the major educational agencies strenuously opposed unifying these functions, urging strict separation between propaganda on the one hand, and cultural relations on the other. They contended that the two approaches involve totally different techniques and that in a combined program propaganda aspects would dominate. It was feared that the temptation to employ educational exchanges directly in the service of our political objectives abroad would be too great under the Smith-Mundt formula and that combining information and cultural relations tended to vitiate the spirit of mutuality and reciprocity upon which such programs were originally built and to jeopardize their acceptance abroad. It is too early to ascertain whether the fears of the educational agencies were justified. Some of them will doubtless be apprehensive over the fact that in the new International Information Administration educational exchange became but one of five coordinate services, the others being devoted to press and publication, motion pictures, broadcasting, and information centers. The reorganization leaves, however, the UNESCO Relations Staff under the Assistant Secretary of State for Public Affairs, whose other functions are concerned primarily with public relations.

Cultural relations activities have also been carried on by other departments in the United States government, some of these going back many years. The United States Department of Agriculture, for example, maintains a substantial international relations program under the Office of Foreign Agricultural Relations, which has for years promoted exchanges of persons and information. This office was tapped very heavily for advice and personnel by UNRRA and the United Nations Food and Agriculture Organization and has also provided indispensable services in connection with the development of the Point Four and Mutual Security programs.

Similarly the Department of Labor, the United States Office of Education and its parent body, the Federal Security Agency, the Department of the Interior, the Library of Congress, and the Smithsonian Institution have fostered long-term programs of cultural relations. Immediately following the war, the War Department (later the Department of the Army) found itself deeply involved in educational and cultural affairs in the occupied countries—Germany, Austria, Japan, and the Ryukyus. More recently the Economic Cooperation Administration, now the Mutual Security Agency, has assumed similar functions.

The extreme decentralization of official cultural relations activities in many federal agencies is extremely confusing at home and almost incomprehensible abroad. It is partially explicable by the lack in the United States of any agency comparable to a ministry of education and cultural affairs which in other countries usually has responsibility both for domestic administration of public schools, higher institutions, and cultural agencies, and for the administration of cultural relations programs abroad. In the United States, of course, education is a function of the states and not of the federal government, with the U. S. Office of Education serving primarily as a fact-finding agency and disseminator of information, also administering certain special educational programs. This has made it easier for separate and sometimes conflicting programs to develop, and for new functions to be assigned to the agency responsible for the conduct of foreign affairs, the Department of State.

VOLUNTARY PROGRAMS

The United States Congress, in establishing the U.S. National Commission for UNESCO, the Fulbright scholarships, and the Smith-Mundt program, recognized the importance of government participation in cultural relations activities, hitherto largely left to private initiative. It had, however, the foresight to recognize officially the continued importance of voluntary initiative, making mandatory the utilization of available private facilities. The whole tenor of these acts and of the implementing legislation and appropriations is that, in cultural affairs especially, the close partnership of government and private effort is essential in view of the sensitive, delicate relationships involved in efforts to facilitate cultural intercourse between peoples. The Congress has thus recognized a distinction between those things which can be done only by governments, or can best be done by governments, and those which are beyond the capacity of official agencies.

The chapters which follow develop this point. It may be

sufficient to suggest here that cultural relations defined as contact of "peoples to peoples" on a basis of mutuality and complete rapport, implies that the political objectives of governments and nations must not be allowed to dominate. To the extent that government information-providing, political, economic, and military programs abroad increase, they must be balanced by ever-increasing stress upon voluntary efforts. To the extent that in recent years the tendency has been toward a vast expansion of federal cultural programs, a parallel expansion of voluntary cultural relations is of the utmost importance. This thesis serves as the foundation of the present volume and of the wide range of activities which it summarizes and attempts to clarify and to strengthen.

3.

Educational Reconstruction: An Example of Cooperative Effort

A CONCRETE ILLUSTRATION of the role that voluntary effort can play in dealing with a specific international problem is found in the work of the Commission for International Educational Reconstruction (CIER) between 1946 and 1949, organized by the American Council on Education with the cooperation of UNRRA, the UNESCO Preparatory Commission, and the Department of State. Through this voluntary agency the postwar cultural needs of the devastated areas and the millions of displaced persons were ascertained, voluntary projects initiated, government programs urged, and interest in UNESCO and international cooperation promoted. During CIER's life, voluntary efforts in international educational reconstruction grew phenomenally. Less than forty organizations reported such projects in 1946, as compared with nearly 400 in 1949. The combined cash value of such programs for the three-year period was approximately $214 million in addition to United States federal programs for similar purposes totaling more than $50 million.

Far more important than the monetary value of this vast effort were its educational and spiritual values. CIER afforded a concrete, dramatic channel whereby American agencies representing literally tens of millions of persons—church members, students, professionals, farmers, members of patriotic, veterans', civic, women's, and fraternal organizations—received direct experience in international relations. Encouraged to develop their own projects in the spirit of UNESCO's slogan of "peoples speaking to peoples," these organizations collected and sent books and other educational materials, provided scholarships, affiliated with groups abroad, organized teaching and technical missions, supported work camps, promoted interchanges in the arts, developed seminars, and endeavored to assist in meeting all sorts of educational and cultural needs.

The vast majority of long-range and permanent projects in international cultural relations described in Part II of this volume had their origin in these educational reconstruction efforts. It has seemed appropriate, therefore, to tell in some detail CIER's story to illustrate the possibilities of voluntary action in international cultural relations.

Other important examples of joint effort in international cultural relations have been reported elsewhere. One of these is the Committee on Educational Reconstruction (recently renamed the Committee on Voluntary International Assistance) of the U.S. National Commission for UNESCO, which took over CIER's remaining functions. Its activities, now particularly centering around the UNESCO Gift Coupon Plan, are reported in publications of UNESCO and the Department of State. Another is the Commission on the Occupied Areas of the American Council on Education, which is fully reported in Council publications, particularly in *An Experiment in International Cultural Relations* by George E. Beauchamp and the present author.

THE SETTING

In one important respect, a gulf wider than the two oceans separates most Americans from their neighbors in Europe and Asia. This gulf is created not so much by physical distance, or difference in race, language, custom, or national aspiration, important as these are. It is created by the almost completely different set of experiences undergone by the American people and those of Europe and Asia during and since the war years. Seven years after the close of the war it is easy for Americans to forget that so wide a gulf in experience still exists.

How can a people on whose cities no bombs ever fell comprehend the suffering, the despair, and often even the resentment of those who experienced night after night of sleepless terror? How can we understand the fear and hate engendered in the hearts of many who are still preoccupied with the daily struggle for physical survival? How can we fully sympathize with the problems of those millions of youth abroad, deprived during the military occupation of all normal educational opportunities, subjected for years to the perverted teachings of totalitarian masters, taught as a matter of patriotic duty to lie, steal, cheat, and even to kill to obtain sufficient food, to protect parents and friends, or to embarrass the enemy?

The account which follows does not provide adequate answers to all, or to any of these questions. It does attempt to show a few of the things that American agencies did in an organized way to provide food for minds as well as bodies in the devastated areas.

EDUCATION AT THE WAR'S END

Educational institutions during a period of war or enemy occupation remain important institutions—less as schools than as buildings. In many smaller communities the school is the only structure suitable for use as barracks or storehouse for armies. Thus, in Greece, France, the Philippines, Yugoslavia, and elsewhere, hundreds of schools were withdrawn from their intended purpose for four or five years, or even longer.

Even where schools were not needed for military purposes, attendance was extremely difficult. Lack of shoes and clothing, lack of fuel and food, kept pupils home during winter months. Male teachers, more generally employed abroad even in elementary schools, were singled out for particular persecution. Many were, of course, killed in the fighting. Many joined the underground. In Norway and other countries, teachers, as community leaders and carriers of the national tradition, were singled out by occupying authorities for special persecution to check the spirit of resistance and break community morale. They were confined in concentration camps, and by tens of thousands, especially in Poland, lost their lives.

Some teachers, of course, remained and tried to carry on against fearful odds. Elementary school classes often included more than 100 pupils. Textbooks were largely destroyed by the occupying armies on the grounds of political inacceptability. Paper, pencils, chalk, blackboards, and school furniture were rapidly used up and could not be replaced. Whenever possible, Quisling teachers were assigned to indoctrinate youth with totalitarian views.

Following the occupation, schools gradually reopened. In many areas, departing armies bombed or burned the school buildings so that they could not serve again as barracks. The chaotic aftermath of the war made the re-establishment of educational opportunity slow and sporadic.

Even with schools reopened, children continued to suffer the effect of war's privations. Millions of orphaned, tuberculous, and crippled children bore tragic testimony to war's horrors. Hundreds of thousands had lost arms and legs from air raids, frostbite, and booby-trap bombs. Undersized children and those suffering otherwise from malnutrition constituted the majority in many regions. The terrors of starvation and of enemy occupation had also left their mark on youthful minds and emotions. Children were restless, nervous, irritable, suspicious, sometimes arrogant, often excessively meek and submissive.[1]

On the other hand, having been forced to assume adult responsibilities during the war years, boys and girls had in many ways matured far beyond their years. They tended to resent mere charity, but demanded an opportunity in no uncertain terms.

Thousands of schools lacked at the war's end equipment of any kind. In whole towns, nearly all schools were windowless, many without roofs. Textbooks and even the simplest of school supplies were lacking. Most communities gave the rebuilding of schools highest priority, even before restoring homes and factories. To make up for education lost during the war years, special summer and week-end classes were inaugurated. Lack of books and writing

[1] For a vivid account of the impact of the war upon children, see *The Teacher and the Postwar Child* by Leonard Kenworthy, based upon UNESCO's initial field study conducted in Greece in 1946 by Mr. Kenworthy and the present author. See also the publications of the Commission for International Educational Reconstruction in the Bibliography.

materials proved a serious handicap, but not a deterrent. Writing and reading could be taught, if necessary, by the scratching of words in the schoolyard dust. Science could be learned from specimens brought in from the fields and woods. The teaching of history, literature, and geography depended mainly upon the memories of the teachers. The presence in most devastated countries of international teams of UNRRA workers lent reality to the teaching of history and geography, providing a living example of that postwar international cooperation which, it was confidently expected, would at long last provide the basis of a durable peace.

Teachers were scarce and poorly trained. Many never returned home. Those who did presented all sorts of handicaps—physical, emotional, professional. Thousands bore the scars of life in concentration camps. All had lost contact with their professions during the war years. Time and facilities for recuperation, reorientation, and retraining were almost totally lacking. Their memories and their ingenuity were often the only materials available to assist them in devising ways of teaching adapted to primitive conditions and to the new physical and psychological handicaps of their pupils.

Adding to their many difficulties, teachers as salaried workers suffered severely from postwar inflation. For example, in Greece, the average teacher's monthly salary of $30.00 in 1946 could scarcely purchase a pair of shoes. In Italy, France, Poland, and particularly China, the economic status of the teacher had sunk below that of the common laborer. For thousands, teaching became of necessity only a part-time profession, combined with all sorts of manual, clerical, and other work.

UNIVERSITIES AND OTHER CULTURAL INSTITUTIONS

To an even greater degree than in America, the university abroad has been a training center for national leaders. It is, therefore, not surprising that the universities—particularly their faculties—were often singled out for special punishment, during both the fighting and occupation. Professors by the hundreds lost their lives, as did thousands of students, just because they were professors and students. University buildings were requisitioned during the occupation and left in seriously damaged condition, stripped of valuable equipment. Great institutions such as the Chekiang University, and the Universities of the Philippines, Caen, Liége, Louvain, Warsaw, Bologna, and Nijmegen were destroyed.

Even more than elementary and secondary education, university instruction was disrupted and disorganized by the war. Lack of buildings, equipment, and trained faculties, as well as unprecedented overcrowding, made postwar reconstruction of university life unbelievably difficult. Especially in such fields as medicine and the natural sciences, faculties were seriously handicapped by lack of contact with the outside world and with new research in their fields during the war years. Technical institutes and schools of agriculture and engineering were forced to offer laboratory instruction without test tubes or microscopes, and to teach agriculture without fertilizers, tractors, or even livestock.

By 1946 the universities were overcrowded, attempting to accommodate several times their prewar enrollments. Yet, students and faculties, exhausted as they were by their struggle against hunger, lack of fuel, and the effects of inflation, repeatedly gave first priority, when asked what types of aid they most needed, to books and educational equipment. Only rarely did they ask first for aid in meeting their urgent physical needs.

Libraries, museums, institutions for adult education and for handicapped children, schools of art and music underwent similar war and postwar experiences. The famous libraries at Louvain, virtually all major libraries in China, the great museums of Berlin, Dresden, Manila, the conservatories of Naples and Palermo—to mention only a few—were gone. Schools for the vastly increased numbers of blind, crippled, and tuberculous children in the Philippines, Greece, Yugoslavia, and elsewhere had been destroyed or badly damaged. Only about one-third of the prewar books remained in Polish school and public libraries. Losses in the Philippines were so overwhelming that a world-wide search was undertaken for duplicates of important historical records and documents on the history of the country. At a time when music, theater, and the creative arts were particularly needed to revive flagging spirits, musical instruments, paints, crayons, drawing paper, and the other necessities were lacking. Of the Braille printing presses in prewar Europe, only a few remained to meet the needs of a blind population which had multiplied to several times its prewar proportions. Vocational rehabilitation of the blind, and of those who had lost limbs, had scarcely begun in 1946.

THE IMMEDIATE TASK IN 1946

Obviously, first consideration during the early postwar period had to be given to emergency feeding and health services, and to the quick re-establishment of the most essential economic processes. The first of the United Nations agencies, UNRRA, was established for this purpose. The indispensable services of this first postwar effort at international collaboration are a matter of record. UNRRA fed the hungry and averted the starvation of millions. It cured disease and prevented the serious epidemics which always have been regarded as the certain aftermath of war. It helped prostrated countries help themselves by providing the means of restoring their own agricultural economies, industries, and transportation systems.

UNRRA was, however, precluded by its basic charter from undertaking direct aid to cultural institutions. It soon became apparent that, if UNRRA's major purposes were to be achieved, it could not utterly disregard the central importance of training and education. Rehabilitation and recovery depended upon trained manpower. UNRRA soon found itself in a tragically ludicrous position. Its charter permitted sending abroad valuable equipment, but a literal interpretation seemed to forbid training personnel to operate or repair equipment. Eventually, this inconsistency was corrected, and health, welfare, agricultural, and industrial rehabilitation services were reinforced by modest instructional programs, mainly in the field. Training centers for the general orientation of all personnel were also introduced.

UNRRA gave official recognition to educational needs when, in 1945, it extended its contributed supplies program to include educational items of all sorts, enabling it to receive and forward books and materials donated by schools, organizations, and individuals. To make certain that these contributed items met a real need and were of sufficient value to justify shipping, UNRRA invited the American Council on Education to serve as its screening agency for educational materials.

During its last two years, UNRRA's belated recognition of the importance of training and cultural rehabilitation went a considerable step further. Fellowships and advanced study grants were offered to selected technicians of the devastated countries, permitting brief periods of study in the United States and other countries less disrupted by the war. This first postwar international fellowships plan stressed highly individualized, primarily non-academic, study and observation. Streamlined refresher courses ranged from six weeks in the case of penicillin technicians, to several months for surgeons, agriculturists, engineers, social workers, and other specialists. It became, somewhat ironically, almost the least controversial program undertaken by UNRRA, although clearly not within the original intent of its charter. When UNRRA concluded its work, its fellowships program was transferred to the United Nations and the specialized agencies, which have continued such exchanges in virtually the same form as that established in 1945.

Despite the few excursions into educational activity cited above, UNRRA was obviously unable to broaden sufficiently the definition of its scope to include a direct approach to educational reconstruction. This was left to other agencies, such as the Council of Allied Ministers of Education, established during the war by the governments in exile in London. This council met regularly to plan postwar intellectual cooperation. It agreed that an intergovernmental educational organization was essential, and that the first task of the new organization should be educational rehabilitation of the devastated countries. Similar recommendations came from many voluntary bodies, particularly in the United

States and Great Britain. These voluntary agencies, led by George
F. Zook of the American Council on Education and William G.
Carr of the National Education Association of the United States,
succeeded in getting recognition of education in the United Nations Charter, signed in 1945 in San Francisco.

In November 1945, a Preparatory Commission for the new
organization, to be known as the United Nations Educational,
Scientific and Cultural Organization, was established in London.
The urgent importance of reconstruction was recognized by this
Commission, but it failed to receive either a sufficiently clear
mandate or the means to embark upon a comprehensive program.
The overwhelming dimensions of the need, the fear of political
domination of the program by some of the member states, the
conflicting conceptions of UNESCO's role, the very small funds
at its disposal, limited the Preparatory Commission's reconstruction program to a very modest fact-gathering service. When
UNESCO was permanently organized in Paris in December 1946,
it gave first priority to educational, scientific, and cultural reconstruction, but was forced to depend for financial support upon
voluntary efforts by governments and private organizations.

A few leading American educators and educational organizations early recognized the plight of their colleagues in the devastated areas. During the winter of 1945–46, George F. Zook, A. J.
Brumbaugh, William G. Carr, and other educational leaders
warned of the grave problem posed by the neglect of postwar educational rehabilitation. Late in 1945, the American Council on
Education called a series of conferences of representatives of
UNRRA, the UNESCO Preparatory Commission, the Department
of State, the National Education Association, and other leading
national educational associations to consider how American voluntary efforts could aid educational and cultural institutions in the
devastated countries. It was brought out at these meetings, and at
a similar one called by UNRRA in connection with its conference
at Atlantic City in February 1946, that, although considerable
progress had been made with general relief and rehabilitation,
educational reconstruction had scarcely begun.

A year after the war's end, virtually none of the thousands of destroyed schools and cultural institutions in Europe and Asia had been rebuilt. Materials were still almost universally lacking. Few new teachers had been trained. Frustration and disillusionment of professional workers, teachers, and students constituted a serious threat to the re-establishment of conditions of peace and security within the several countries and among the various nations. Major contributions from governments of so-called donor, non-devastated countries seemed out of the question in the light of large commitments to UNRRA. The United States government, and several others, insisted that initiative be left entirely to voluntary agencies. Coordinated private effort could, it was asserted, meet a substantial part of the need, greatly sustain morale in devastated areas, and afford a strong basis of grass-roots support for needed legislative action.

The American Council on Education accordingly sought the aid of the Carnegie Corporation and received a small initial grant to establish a Commission for International Educational Reconstruction. In several other countries relatively spared by the war, similar efforts were made soon thereafter, more largely under government auspices, but including also significant voluntary projects, such as that of the Canadian Council for Reconstruction through UNESCO.

The impression should not be left that the devastated countries had completely neglected their educational rehabilitation prior to 1946. On the contrary, heroic efforts at self-help had been made. UNRRA missions reported with amazement the eagerness with which villagers in Greece, Norway, Italy, and other countries contributed time, effort, and their limited resources to rebuild local schools. They were equally surprised at the high priority given by the unfortunate millions of displaced persons to immediate resumption of educational programs. A Displaced Persons University was established in Munich's Deutsches Museum. By 1945, the Charles University in Prague was already overcrowded several times beyond its normal capacity, students alternating in the use of the few heated study rooms. Scientists, artists, librarians, and writers were encouraged by their governments to resume careers interrupted by the war. The respect for learning which has for centuries characterized Europe and Asia had survived the holocaust. Americans returning from relief work or from military service abroad reported an astonishing and encouraging intellectual vitality, considering the experience which the nations had undergone.

This was the setting for the American voluntary effort.

CIER's Scope

The demand for CIER's creation came jointly from private, governmental, and intergovernmental sources. UNRRA, the UNESCO Preparatory Commission, and the Department of State specifically requested the American Council on Education to act on the strength of the initiative which its president and vice-president had already taken in calling a series of consultative meetings, and the encouraging response to them. Small grants were secured by the Council from the Carnegie Corporation and later from other sources. The Council administered CIER's funds, appointed the members of the commission from among heads of the leading educational associations, selected the director, provided office space, and lent its full facilities to CIER's conferences, publications, and other programs. Therefore, although CIER remained nominally independent, it was for all practical purposes a Council project.[2]

[2] The membership and staff of the commission were as follows: *chairman:* T. G. Pullen, Jr., state superintendent of Maryland schools, for the National Council of Chief State School Officers; *vice-chairman:* A. J. Brumbaugh, vice-president, for the American Council of Education; Lyle W. Ashby, Division of Publications, National Education Association, for the Educational Press Association; Lawrence L. Bethel, president, New Haven Junior College, for the American Association of Junior Colleges; Livingston L. Blair, vice-chairman for School and College Activities for the American Red Cross; William G. Carr, associate secretary, for the National Education Association; L. H. Dennis, executive secretary, American Vocational Association; Stephen Duggan and later Laurence Duggan, director, Institute of International Education; Milton S. Eisenhower, president, Kansas State College, and later, William S. Carlson, president, University of Delaware, for the Association of Land-Grant Colleges and Universities; W.L.W. Field, chairman, National Council of Independent Schools; Rayford W. Logan, professor of history, Howard University, and later Thomas G. Henderson, dean, Virginia Union University, for the Association of Colleges and Secondary Schools for Negroes; Msgr. F. G. Hochwalt, secretary general,

The sponsorship and membership of CIER, and its very name, suggested a stress upon educational needs, particularly those of schools and higher institutions. CIER gradually broadened its scope to include almost all forms of cultural, moral, and psychological assistance, but because its resources remained limited, it continued to give special stress to educational problems, broadly defined.

In defining its time scope, CIER recognized that provision of food, clothing, shelter, and health service had prior claim. It was mainly concerned with the third of the three stages of the postwar timetable in devastated countries—relief, rehabilitation, and reconstruction. However, it recognized the possibility and the *necessity* of combining educational and moral assistance, whenever possible, with the offering of relief and rehabilitation aid. Voluntary basic relief projects, even after World War I, had demonstrated that even the distribution of food can have long-term cultural values, if sensitively administered.

National Catholic Educational Association; Mary E. Leeper, executive secretary, Association for Childhood Education; Cornelius Krusé, executive director, and Waldo G. Leland, director emeritus, American Council of Learned Societies; N. L. Engelhardt, associate superintendent of schools, New York City, and later W. H. Lemmel, superintendent of schools, Baltimore, Maryland, for the American Association of School Administrators; Kathryn McHale, general director, American Association of University Women; Carl H. Milam, executive secretary, American Library Association; J. Earl Moreland, president, Randolph-Macon College, for the Association of American Colleges; Edward O'Connor, executive assistant, National Catholic Welfare Conference, War Relief Services; Charlotte E. Owen, executive secretary, American Council of Voluntary Agencies for Foreign Service, Inc.; W. W. Pierson, administrative dean, University of North Carolina, for the Association of American Universities; Wilfred H. Ringer, professor of education, Tufts College, for the National Association of Secondary-School Principals; Agnes Samuelson, chairman of Committee on School Education, National Congress of Parents and Teachers; Ralph Himstead, general secretary, and later George Pope Shannon, associate secretary, American Association of University Professors; George Shuster, president, Hunter College, for the World Student Service Fund; Paul V. Sangren, president, Western Michigan College of Education; H. A. Sprague, president, New Jersey State Teachers College, Montclair; Harold Benjamin, dean, College of Education, University of Maryland, the last three successively for the American Association of Colleges for Teacher Education; Herman B Wells, president, Indiana University, National Association of State Universities.

Staff: Harold E. Snyder, director; Robert E. Stanforth, assistant director; Margretta S. Austin, staff associate; Rebecca Shedd, Florence Gillham, and Margaret Markley, secretaries. *Executive Committee:* Messrs. Pullen, Brumbaugh, Carr, Dennis, Moreland, and Snyder.

The duration of CIER's task was hard to establish at the outset. Its members and staff insisted that it should be regarded as temporary, that it should work itself out of a job as soon as possible. While reconstruction must clearly continue for many years in some areas, CIER, as an emergency agency, should encourage each cooperating group to develop its own approach. If, after the two years initially agreed upon as the length of the venture, further coordination was needed, a new, more permanent type of service, stressing long-term cultural relations, should be developed. It was hoped that by the time the most urgent reconstruction phase had passed, the U.S. National Commission for UNESCO would be strong enough to take over coordination of some of the remaining reconstruction projects, and that government programs would have been developed to meet many of the remaining needs.

CIER insisted from the first that it was concerned with all countries and peoples suffering from the devastation of war. This caused some difficulty. UNRRA, which offered CIER its shipping facilities, its reports concerning needs, and other invaluable assistance, dealt with all war-devastated areas, except the ex-enemy countries of Germany and Japan, which soon became the special responsibilities of the United States. UNRRA could not help CIER's work in those countries. UNESCO was primarily concerned with serving its own member states which did not yet, in 1946–48, include Germany, Japan, Indonesia, or several of the worst-devastated countries of Europe. UNRRA was eager for CIER's help in displaced persons camps, but UNESCO did not include DP's within its scope.

UNESCO had been expected from the beginning to provide information concerning needs and to follow up CIER's relatively short-term assignment. Since the American effort was, in fact, part of a world-wide campaign under UNESCO's leadership, it seemed awkward indeed to have to define CIER's role more broadly than UNESCO's interest in educational reconstruction. Nevertheless, this was done as a matter of humanitarian principle. CIER from the beginning asserted its concern for *all* devastated areas and *all* peoples suffering educational lacks as a result of the war, including displaced persons, occupied areas, virtually all of Europe, and much of Asia. The freedom to take needed action, regardless of such extraneous factors as the membership or nonmembership of a nation in a particular intergovernmental organization, is obviously one of the great advantages enjoyed by a voluntary agency.

After field investigations of needs by its staff, by UNRRA, by the various governments, eventually by UNESCO, and particularly by American and international voluntary agencies working abroad, CIER defined the following types of activity as representing high priorities in 1946:

1. Basic expendable educational supplies and materials (for the worst-devastated areas only).
2. More durable educational and scientific equipment, particularly that which was conducive to self-help.
3. Printed materials, particularly in technical fields.
4. Fellowships and study grants, especially for mature individuals in positions of established responsibility in fields marked by exceptional technical advances during and since the war.
5. Advisory, teaching, and technical missions.
6. Work camps and other voluntary service projects stressing joint action and self-help.
7. Food, clothing, medical supplies, and other general relief as related to educational needs. (Stress upon educational needs distinguished CIER's emphasis from that of other coordinating efforts in the relief field.)

As time went on, other forms of assistance were encouraged, eventually including almost every type of service clearly emphasizing the meeting of cultural and educational needs, including those relating to moral and spiritual rehabilitation.

EXPRESSING MORAL AND SPIRITUAL VALUES

As indicated above, CIER defined its scope broadly. It was concerned not only with material needs, technical training, and psychological rehabilitation; it was also concerned with the far more subtle factor of promoting moral and spiritual values. While more difficult of precise definition, these values were sought in one form or another in almost every project.

It was early recognized that the war-stricken youth looked to the United States for more than physical assistance. It demanded evidence that we recognized its humanity. It sought from us signs of faith in the future. Rehabilitation of the spirit could be quite as important as rehabilitation of the body.

CIER and its associated organizations recognized that they were working in an area of such vast need that, at best, voluntary efforts could be only symbols—concrete expressions of the good will and humanitarian intent of the American people. This made it of the utmost importance that basic moral and spiritual values be reflected in all educational activities. At the same time, since objectives such as these cannot be precisely defined, their form of expression had to be left largely to each voluntary organization. This also presented certain dangers by opening the door to claims of moral and spiritual values for some projects of dubious value as educational reconstruction. Without questioning their importance, it was, for example, considered beyond CIER's scope to recognize as educational reconstruction religious or missionary efforts. Basic physical relief similarly belonged in a separate category, although often having a direct bearing upon educational reconstruction. The drawing of lines such as these is one of the hardest tasks of a coordinating agency.

EDUCATIONAL AND CULTURAL RELATIONS

Despite its emergency nature, it would have been strange indeed if an agency so deeply rooted in American and international educational experience had not stressed long-term values. CIER included within its own understanding of its mandate two long-range purposes: (1) to effect the closest possible working relationship between American organizations and UNESCO, and between voluntary agencies in the United States and those in other countries; and (2) to utilize reconstruction activities as a means of fostering mutual international and intercultural understanding through development of permanent interchanges of materials, persons, and ideas.

Many attempts at educating for internationalism begin and end at the verbal, conceptual level. Courses, discussions, reading,

lectures, correspondence can obviously contribute to clear thinking and effective action. They may even lead to constructive activity. But they do not usually provide mutually satisfying international contacts. Basic relief projects involve action, but are
strictly limited in the degree to which direct permanent relationships between large numbers of persons can be fostered.

Educational reconstruction projects provided an *action* approach
to international understanding. They permitted enrichment of
the educational experience and long-term cultural relations by
fostering direct ties with people abroad. The depth and sincerity
of international convictions are often put to their severest test
when translated into action terms. Reconstruction projects provided a channel for getting agencies, institutions, and individuals
beyond the stage of verbalization. They probed the capacity of
organized groups to respond to needs expressed not exclusively
in terms of physical human suffering, but also as long-term
human and cultural values. CIER therefore stressed long-range
contacts. In so doing, it helped American voluntary agencies make
the transition from immediate postwar preoccupation with
material aid to more fundamental forms of reconstruction.

WHAT EDUCATIONAL RECONSTRUCTION WAS NOT

CIER's reports and publications and public statements made by
its staff and members endeavored repeatedly to warn against three
common misconceptions of reconstruction. These were, stated
negatively:

1. *Educational reconstruction was not charity in the narrow
sense of that term.* It was enlightened self-interest. It was also a
very partial repayment of a debt incurred by every American to
those who bore the brunt of war's destruction. The spirit of
educational reconstruction had to be kept free from any suggestion
of condescension, implication of pauperization of the recipient,
or reflection of the "Lady Bountiful" attitude.

2. *Educational reconstruction was not a one-way street, that is,
a matter of giving without receiving anything in return.* It was a
contribution to world recovery and stability, aimed particularly

at the younger generation abroad, whose attitudes and well-being may largely determine the attainment of a peaceful world for our own youth as well. If lack of opportunity, frustration, and embitterment increased susceptibility to totalitarian blandishments, our own security was at stake. In addition, Americans could gain much in understanding of world affairs, in the arts, in terms of human values, and in innumerable other ways from direct contact with other cultures.

3. *Educational reconstruction could not, and should not, seek to remake the world in the American pattern.* However excellent American education and social institutions may be for us, cultural patterns could not readily be transplanted or imposed upon others. It was, however, feasible and appropriate, to offer to share the benefit of our experience and development in those fields which others recognize as relevant to the solution of problems they are facing.

DEFINING NEEDS

Of first importance in the reconstruction effort was the obtaining of accurate and complete information concerning the needs of the devastated countries. No single authoritative source for such information existed in 1946. By 1948 UNESCO was beginning to provide more and better reporting on needs. Even then, however, it remained necessary to supplement this information from other sources.

Considerable information concerning educational needs was available to CIER from the beginning through UNRRA's widespread organization throughout the world. CIER's director, previously director of training for UNRRA, brought from the latter agency a considerable body of detailed information on needs. This he was able to supplement by field experience during the summer of 1946, when Leonard Kenworthy, of the secretariat of the UNESCO Preparatory Commission, and he undertook UNESCO's first field survey, a study of the educational needs of Greece. This was followed by briefer visits to several other European countries in 1946 and 1947. CIER's assistant director also conducted several field studies in 1947. Its chairman, vice-chairman, and more than half of the members of the commission visited war-devastated areas and submitted reports. Reports of United States government agencies, especially those of the Department of State, the Department of Agriculture, the Army Department, and the U.S. Office of Education added valuable information. Foreign governments, especially their embassies and ministries of education, contributed to the fund of knowledge concerning needs. Books and periodicals, American and foreign, were also collected and studied.

Aside from direct field studies by staff and members, the most important and objective single source of information concerning educational and cultural lacks came from the leading American and international voluntary agencies, such as the Red Cross, the World Student Service Fund, the United Service to China, Greek War Relief, CARE, Church World Service, the National Catholic Welfare Conference, the various service organizations such as those of the Unitarians, Brethren, Friends, and Jewish groups, and the educational organizations with world-wide contacts such as the National Education Association, the American Association of University Women, and the Institute of International Education.

As a result of CIER's many channels of information, UNESCO's early inability to report needs promptly and accurately did not prove a serious handicap. By November 1946, when CIER called its first National Conference on International Educational Reconstruction, it was possible to list the major categories of need with complete assurance. UNESCO's own later classification of needs followed very closely that of CIER. Both stated needs primarily in terms of types of possible service—publications, equipment, educational and technical advisory service, fellowships and study grants, work camps and other self-help approaches, and food and clothing for teachers and other professional workers. Such classifications had the advantage of permitting needs to be translated easily into definite, recognizable services and projects.

However, additional quantitative and qualitative information concerning changing educational needs soon proved essential. CIER, with a staff never exceeding three professional persons, lacked adequate facilities for keeping its information up to date, and UNESCO's early development was slow. Eventually, vivid quantitative information became available through UNESCO's *Books of Needs*. But during CIER's entire existence, no adequate qualitative analysis was ever available. The "qualitative approach" here refers to the identification of those particularly sensitive points in the educational recovery and development of a country and an institution which could provide the "grease where the squeak is," the spark that leads to self-help, the cornerstone of the whole educational edifice. Such qualitative analyses might have given a far clearer picture of the distinctive role of voluntary effort, as compared with those things which can, and must, be left to governments. Good qualitative studies could have provided clearer priorities among the many things and services needed.

METHOD

CIER defined its role as that of stimulating and coordinating desirable action. It emphasized that it was not, and should not become, an operating agency. It urged organizations and institutions developing projects to utilize operating machinery of existing agencies. When no satisfactory operating machinery was available to meet a particular need, CIER helped to strengthen established agencies. In a very few cases it assisted in creating totally new agencies when none existed capable of meeting a pressing need.

CIER's method was to stress activity by American organizations geared to their own competence, interests, and resources. Organizations were encouraged to define projects within the spirit of UNESCO, without depending too heavily upon the then strictly limited information-giving and operating facilities of UNESCO and of the United States government. This approach was heartily supported both by UNESCO and the Department of State. It enabled UNESCO to share in the prestige, both in the United States and abroad, accruing from the vast growth in reconstruction effort, at a time when all United Nations agencies were still in the early stages of development. If UNESCO had been swamped with requests for information and advice far beyond its capacity, or for operating assistance which it could not provide competently, it could have lost public confidence. CIER's approach served, however, to establish in the minds of both Americans and nationals of other UNESCO states the concept of UNESCO as an action agency, not an instrumentality for mere discussion and passing of resolutions.

CIER stressed putting American organizations to work, each in its own way. This precluded a single, central public appeal for funds for four reasons: (1) Such an appeal would have run, especially during 1946 and 1947, directly into competition with the still-urgent campaigns for food, clothing, and other basic relief of the principal operating agencies, upon whose response and operating machinery CIER knew it must ultimately depend. (2) By avoiding competition with these agencies, CIER was able to work with them and gradually assist them in developing educational and long-range cultural projects to supplement their relief and other programs. (3) Both UNESCO and CIER lacked the field staff, the basic financing, and other facilities essential to conducting sound campaigns for funds. Above all, both lacked personnel for distributing funds wisely and for supervising the use made of them. (4) The impersonality of huge cash appeals, the donor's difficulty in following the contribution through to the recipient, made such an approach educationally questionable.

Since 1949, when CIER terminated, considerable progress has been made in strengthening UNESCO's facilities for handling such programs, reducing somewhat the force of some of the above considerations. The essential principles behind them, however, still apply. Actually, CIER compromised at one point with its reluctance to assume operating responsibility and its hesitancy to sponsor direct collection of funds. Through its principal sponsoring agency, the American Council on Education, and in cooperation with the National Association of Secondary-School Principals and the American Association of Junior Colleges, a special appeal was directed to the graduating classes of American colleges and high schools to establish "living class memorials" in the form of class contributions for an educational reconstruction project, either utilizing an established operating agency, or contributing directly to UNESCO's Reconstruction Fund. A certificate suitable for framing was sent to each participating school or college. This unique project, first conceived by Livingston L. Blair, vice-president, American Red Cross, and a member of CIER, yielded in 1948 over $72,000 from schools and colleges in forty-four states, the District of Columbia, Hawaii, Alaska, and Puerto Rico.

It quickly became apparent that the twenty-seven major educational organizations officially represented on CIER by no means constituted its sole support. More than one hundred agencies responded to the call for the First National Conference on International Educational Reconstruction held in Washington in November 1946. One hundred and sixty agencies participated in the Second National Conference a year later. Nearly three times this number of organizations was reached by CIER's publications, by correspondence, and by staff consultation services.

CIER offered advice and assistance to voluntary organizations in planning projects, and to the Department of State and UNESCO. These took the form of consultant service, numerous addresses and articles by the staff, and participation of the director as adviser to UNESCO conferences in London, Mexico City, and Paris. The chairman, vice-chairman, and assistant director also advised UNESCO conferences, as did several of its members. CIER conducted a modest publications program, beginning with the joint publication with UNESCO of *Going to School in War Devastated Countries* by Leonard Kenworthy; the *CIER Handbook* and its annual supplements reporting the extent of voluntary efforts for educational reconstruction, listing participating agencies, and describing their projects; publication of *The Bulletin of CIER*, semimonthly during 1946–47 and monthly during 1947–48 and 1948–49; and, finally, joint publication with UNESCO of *It's Yours for the Giving* by Margretta S. Austin. CIER's mailing list for *The Bulletin* and other current information totaled at its peak more than 2,500.

Another partial exception to CIER's nonoperating policy was its organization in the spring and summer of 1948 and 1949 of the CIER Cooperative Project in International Education. This was a joint effort, shared by ten organizations—the American Junior Red Cross, the National Education Association, the American Association of Colleges for Teacher Education, the American Association of University Women, Delta Kappa Gamma, the Department of Classroom Teachers of the National Education Association, the Association for Childhood Education, the American Library Association, the West Virginia Classroom Teachers Association, and the Department of the Army. The project brought together educators from fifteen countries of Europe and Asia to study and observe developments in American education relating to their fields and to participate in seminars in international education, in 1948 at the University of Maryland, in 1949 at Syracuse University.

RELATIONS WITH GOVERNMENT

As noted above, CIER worked in very close association with the various United States government agencies, especially the U.S. National Commission for UNESCO, which specifically designated CIER in 1946, 1947, and 1948 as the agency to which it looked to transmit to the American public UNESCO's reconstruction appeal.

Less well known, perhaps, is the part played by CIER in legislative action, including the Fulbright Act, the Smith-Mundt Act, and appropriations for educational exchanges and other cultural programs, and for the development of educational and cultural aspects of United States Military Government in Germany, Austria, Japan, and Ryukyus. When legislative action on such items as the above was pending, CIER collected materials for hearings, submitted reports to individual members of Congress, and urged testimony and correspondence by cooperating agencies. Twice, when the appropriations for the Smith-Mundt Act were threatened, information supplied by CIER to civic, business, religious, and educational organizations resulted in prompt and vigorous representations to Congress from many parts of the country. The wholly voluntary direction of an international project such as

CIER permits a freedom of action not available to official agencies.

One of CIER's last acts in 1949 was to direct, through the president of the American Council on Education, a letter to the ministers of education of all countries involved in the Marshall Plan. This letter, prepared with the full knowledge and consent of the Economic Cooperation Administration, called attention to the possible availability of the ECA funds for educational reconstruction activity relating directly to the aims of that agency, permitting the building of vocational schools and technical institutes, and the provision of many types of needed training.

CIER also played an active part, at the request of Canadian educational agencies, in the development of the Canadian Council for Reconstruction through UNESCO in 1947, and worked closely with this organization. The Canadian Council reciprocated by making available to CIER its film on educational reconstruction, *Hungry Minds*.

RESULTS

CIER's accomplishments may be judged only partially in tangible, statistical terms. However, the figures are impressive. Several excellent voluntary programs of educational reconstruction antedated CIER's birth in 1946. However, CIER was able to identify less than forty organizations engaged in such work early in 1946. This number had grown by the time CIER made its first national survey in 1947 to 153 organizations reporting specific projects and to approximately 400 before CIER concluded its work in July 1949. The *CIER Handbooks* and their supplements accounted either directly, or through listings of groups of co-operating agencies, for most of these but necessarily omitted hundreds of local organizations not affiliated with, or reporting through, national organizations and left out many schools and colleges conducting independent projects. Through the national organizations alone, including some of the largest in the country, it is estimated that tens of millions of Americans played at least some small part in world educational reconstruction.

The dollar value of this effort, including cash contributions, gifts in kind, cost of shipping and administration reported to CIER totaled $62 million in 1946, $88 million in 1947, and $64 million in 1948. Because of CIER's termination, comparable figures for 1949 and the years following are not available. The combined figure of $214 million for the period of CIER's activity, derived from the above estimates, is doubtless too low. As had been anticipated, a decline in contributions for educational reconstruction (although proportionately far less than the decline in giving for overseas relief) occurred during the latter half of 1948 and 1949. However, it is doubtful whether educational reconstruction efforts dropped as low as suggested by a partial survey by UNESCO, covering only 120 organizations. This showed a combined contribution in 1949 of less than $24 million. Changes in UNESCO's program and method of conducting its program made it impossible to gather comparable figures.

Still dealing in quantitative terms, the growth in response to CIER's, and later to COA's, national conferences afforded evidence that interest in international educational projects continued to grow, even after actual cash value of projects had declined. The first CIER conference in 1946 attracted approximately 220 representatives of more than 100 organizations and agencies, and the 1947 conference 210 leaders of 160 agencies. In 1949 a similar National Conference on the Occupied Countries drew 470 registrants from 200 agencies, and the 1950 conference nearly 700 from about the same number of agencies, although these two conferences were limited to four countries, and a registration fee was charged.

On the far more important qualitative side, a few results are tangible, the rest merely fairly intelligent guesses. Some of these results have already been mentioned; others are cited in chapter 4, on voluntary efforts. Perhaps the best evidence of CIER's effectiveness is in the list of cultural relations programs cited in Part II, most of these stemming from reconstruction projects. At no time, to be sure, did CIER claim to be responsible for all of the efforts reported to it by hundreds of cooperating organizations. Much fine work would have been done if CIER had never existed.

A few quotations from persons who observed CIER closely may

be justified. At its ninth, and final, meeting in March 1949, Waldo
G. Leland, vice-chairman of the U.S. National Commission for
UNESCO and director emeritus of the American Council of
Learned Societies, said:

We have stated many times that the nature of the services of CIER
has contributed much to the National Commission. CIER was organized previous to the formation of the U.S. National Commission. We
were able to turn over to CIER a chapter which would have been most
difficult for us to accomplish. If it had not been for CIER, I am afraid
the record of the United States, in a matter which touches on a very
serious problem, would have been smaller and much less glorious than
it has been—perhaps even inglorious. On behalf of the UNESCO program, I want to express very deep gratitude to CIER for bearing some
of the most important burdens that we had to carry at that time and
which we could not have carried by ourselves.

We should also express appreciation to the various groups and organizations which have put up the money and done the work. While coordination has been successful due to the efficiency of the staff of CIER,
the individual organizations have done a remarkable job. Efforts in the
field of reconstruction here are greater than in the rest of the world put
together.

The chairman of the U.S. National Commission for UNESCO,
Milton S. Eisenhower, wrote on March 8, 1949, to the chairman of
CIER, "In my judgment, support of the CIER program is the
best opportunity offered to American education to work effectively
for peace." Peter Edson, nationally syndicated columnist, devoted
two articles to CIER. Speaking of CIER's two grants from the
Carnegie Corporation, he wrote, "It was probably one of the best
$100,000 investments ever made."

Ambassador Vassili Dendramis of Greece wrote in April 1948
as follows: "I want you to know that all voluntary aid projects are
deeply appreciated by my government because, beyond their
value in dollars and the importance of the needs they fill, they
also carry a moral assistance of inestimable value—proportionately
far greater than any governmental aid. In the adverse circumstances confronting Greece today this moral factor should, in my
opinion, be rated very high indeed."

Ambassador V. K. Wellington Koo of China wrote: "It goes

without saying that your generosity is deeply appreciated by our people and that your efforts will go a long way toward developing good will and understanding between our two peoples."

From N. Margue, Minister of National Education, Luxembourg: "Permit me to congratulate your continent for the generosity with which it has aided in healing the wounds of war in Europe, generosity which will never be forgotten in our country. . . . I have high hope that the good will and understanding among peoples, which your Commission is concerned with promotion of, will increase greatly the likelihood of establishing lasting peace throughout the world."

From Ambassador Baron Silvercruys of Belgium: "Whilst providing badly needed assistance, these organizations go a long way in fostering better understanding and closer friendship between nations."

Similar letters were received from General Lucius D. Clay, Commanding General, U. S. Military Government for Germany; Lt. Gen. John K. Hodge, Commander, U. S. Army forces in Korea; and the Ambassadors or Ministers of Education of Italy, Denmark, Austria, Philippine Republic, Poland, and Czechoslovakia.

4.

The Role of Voluntary Action

Behind the vast American voluntary efforts of the postwar years is the assumption that the task of conducting world affairs is one in which governments, intergovernmental agencies, and private groups all must share. This need for "three-cornered" participation extends to virtually every form of international relations. Even the conduct of political and economic affairs, sometimes assumed to be the business of governments, depends in the last analysis upon all three elements. The formulation of foreign policy in a democracy cannot be left to a foreign office, a military, or even a Congress. To be effective and durable, it must reflect the basic outlook and aspirations of a whole people, as clarified in thousands of large and small discussions and in the work of hundreds of organizations.

A foreign policy which does not express the intentions of a people as a whole is a mere temporary formulation, certain to be repudiated or drastically revised. Therein lies much of the genius and vitality of a democratic society. In contrast, the policy-making process in totalitarian countries need reflect no such concern for the popular will.

Vast international economic programs, such as the Marshall Plan, depend equally upon the cooperation of the people, as expressed through nongovernmental action. The success of ECA was in no small measure due to the willingness of American business and American labor to join with government in meeting an international crisis, and to the readiness of the whole American people to submit to the necessary taxation and to make other essential sacrifices.

ASSISTANCE PROJECTS

Foreign assistance programs of major proportions obviously require administrative machinery available only to governments or to intergovernmental agencies, and must be supported from tax funds. But even official emergency assistance programs can be strengthened by supplementary voluntary action. Political tags can too easily—rightly or wrongly—become attached abroad to bilateral acts of governments, however humanitarian their intent. Due in part to their size and scope, official assistance projects are often necessarily characterized by highly impersonal administration. Governments subject to sudden internal changes, to legislative pressures, or to annual appropriations of funds can make only relatively short-term commitments. Their technique is inherently "government-to-government." These factors too often reduce the value of official programs as true expressions of the humanitarian spirit of a whole people.

Voluntary assistance projects are relatively free from such disadvantages, although obviously subject to equally serious limitations. They may suffer from restricted resources and facilities, command less direct access to accurate sources of information concerning needs, and are sometimes inclined to subordinate assistance to other purposes. Private agencies often have, however, greater elasticity. They can more readily translate their assistance projects into vehicles for building lasting cooperative relations. They can often utilize their practical experience in foreign fields to build sound support at home for needed government programs. They can more easily achieve relationships abroad in which "peoples speak to peoples." Such coordinating agencies as the State Department's Advisory Committee on Voluntary Foreign Aid and the private American Council of Voluntary Agencies for Foreign Service, and scores of other agencies have conducted their programs in such manner as to capitalize these assets of private endeavor.

Intergovernmental action, supplementing, complementing, and coordinating action by nations, may often be more efficient than that of individual governments. The urgent postwar tasks of feeding persons cut off from food supplies, of protecting and caring for refugees, and of restoring transportation and the other sinews of agricultural and industrial rehabilitation, demanded joint international effort. Whatever may be the current criticisms of UNRRA, that agency suceeded to an astonishing degree in its primary responsibilities of preventing starvation and epidemic, and of caring for and speedily repatriating the vast majority of displaced persons. The alternative to UNRRA would have been the creation of a complex series of competing national programs. The resulting chaos, so fraught with possibilities of political friction, could actually have been cruel and dangerous. On the other hand, to have left relief and rehabilitation wholly to private organizations might have had even more disastrous consequences.

The list of fields of endeavor in which joint international action is obviously necessary in the interest of each individual nation, including our own, is too long and too obvious to repeat here. The essential point is that governmental, intergovernmental, and private effort each have a part to play in the meeting of urgent world problems—even those which are essentially political and economic, and especially those in which assistance to and relations with other peoples are at stake.

Postwar assistance programs demonstrated vividly not only the necessity of this triangular cooperation, but also its practical possibilities. UNRRA utilized both governments and voluntary agencies in nearly every operation. To cite only a few instances, medical teaching missions, educational services in displaced persons camps, shipment of heifers to cattle-depleted countries, and procurement of clothing and equipment all depended, at least in part, upon private action, coordinated by UNRRA. The practice of using private agencies, not only in operations, but in policy formulation as well, has extended to the United Nations and its specialized agencies. The International Red Cross and other groups have administered Arab refugee camps for the United Nations. The Unitarian Service Committee has sent abroad, with the help of the intergovernmental agencies, outstanding medical and dental professors. Many private groups have cooperated with the International Refugee Organization, the United Nations International Children's Emergency Fund, and in U.N. technical assistance programs. The latter have involved coordinate, dovetailing, government projects, such as our Point Four and the British Colombo Plan, which, in turn, utilize nongovernment groups for advice, operating assistance, evaluation, and development of long-term relationships with countries helped.

CULTURAL PROJECTS

In the highly sensitive and complex field of international cultural relations, the need for this three-way approach is particularly evident. The very inclusion in the United Nations Charter of several references to the central importance of educational, scientific, and cultural cooperation resulted from a grass-roots demand by voluntary educational agencies of many nations, vigorously expressed at the historic San Francisco conference in 1945. The establishment of UNESCO stemmed in no small part from the efforts of private educational agencies in the United States which finally secured United States government backing for the new organization. UNESCO's ability to translate its educational reconstruction and other programs quickly into action terms has likewise been dependent upon voluntary support.

Such coordinating organizations as the Commission for International Educational Reconstruction, mobilizing scores of educational, civic, professional, religious, labor, and other organized groups, produced requisite popular support for constructive congressional actions in international cultural relations. The Fulbright Act, the Smith-Mundt Act, and the legislation establishing a U.S. National Commission for UNESCO all depended in large measure upon vigorous voluntary action. The Commission on the Occupied Areas, working in close collaboration with a similar group of private agencies, developed public awareness and support during the occupation of Germany, Austria, Japan, and the Ryukyus, for greater emphasis in government programs upon educational and cultural values and relations. This private agency advised both government and voluntary agencies, developed and administered many private and official projects, actively assisted in securing adequate government appropriations. In addition, COA fostered long-term relationships such as affiliations between American schools and colleges and those in the occupied countries—one among scores of its activities clearly beyond the capacity of government alone.[1]

"SIGHT-RAISING"

Private agencies are often freer than government agencies to emphasize joint international action in the national interest. COA was able, for example, to urge utilization of UNESCO in government educational projects in the occupied countries, pointing out the value for certain specific purposes of supplementing United States–German interchange with less expensive and sometimes more productive study by Germans in other democratic countries. This required changes in policies relating to the use of United States government funds. It entailed overcoming legalistic interpretations of congressional appropriations, revamping "standard government operating procedures," and even, in a few instances, coping with short-sighted ultra-nationalism on the part of key officials. Such initiative had to be taken outside of government.

"Sight-raising" educational work can be one of the major contributions of private agencies to government and to intergovernmental agencies. Nongovernmental organizations are free to advise, experiment, criticize, urge legislation, build public opinion, and often to tap professional services not so readily available to government. The history of many of our major domestic reforms reveals that many, if not most, were produced by intensive, unofficial efforts. The abolition of slavery, the achievement of woman suffrage, and old-age assistance (to mention only a few) resulted from prodigious organized private activity. The people are often ready and able to respond to human needs which governments are either slow to recognize or unable to cope with until political opinion has sufficiently matured.

Voluntary agencies can serve as the conscience of a democratic society, both in international and in domestic affairs. Even in the

[1] See *An Experiment in International Cultural Relations: A Report of the Staff of the Commission on the Occupied Areas,* by Harold E. Snyder and George E. Beauchamp (Washington: American Council on Education, 1951).

framing of foreign policy, private organizations play an active part, supplemented increasingly by research and scientific analysis in our universities and by the vast discussion programs of such local groups as world affairs councils and women voters organizations.

One must hastily add that by no means all private groups, among the many speaking out today on international affairs, can be classified "sight-raisers." As in every other field, special-interest agencies abound in foreign relations. Those with frank or concealed ulterior motives are often among the first to express themselves on international problems and programs and to try to influence government action. Even those groups with thoroughly humanitarian objectives may be very badly advised, overly emotional or sentimental, or reflect fuzzy thinking. Some private organizations are misled by the strong biases or limited insights of a few individual leaders. Organizations may be as subject as governments to sudden changes in policies, programs, and personnel, especially if their officers change from year to year.

Skilled government officials can distinguish among organizations of various types, utilize the most reliable, and skillfully counter the irresponsible. However, the extreme diversity among private agencies and the time and effort required to differentiate among them, provides a convenient excuse at times to those few officials who wish to carry out their own programs with a minimum of public interference. On the other hand, some pressure groups are so vocal, so demanding, so intemperate of expression, that timid officials find it expedient to drop projects entirely rather than run the risk of political repercussions.

Voluntary Coordinating Agencies and Government

To utilize the best private resources and eliminate what is biased or unsound, government has several approaches. One is to establish, either by law or by executive action, official advisory committees or commissions. Another is to recognize the initiative of nongovernmental agencies in establishing their own coordinating machinery, broadly representative of the major private interests concerned with a particular policy or program.

Both of these approaches are prevalent in the field of international cultural relations. The U.S. National Commission for UNESCO, the Department of State's Advisory Commission on Information and Advisory Commission on Educational Exchange are official bodies, established by law. They are designed to be broadly representative of the major interests in their fields of endeavor and are essentially nonoperating. The UNESCO Commission advises the government both on matters concerned with UNESCO's program throughout the world, and on the implementation of UNESCO's program within the United States. The two advisory commissions, mentioned above, established under the Smith-Mundt Act, are responsible for policies respecting the government's programs of overseas information and educational exchange. All three agencies are staffed by secretariats within the Department of State. In addition, innumerable special committees, some permanent, others *ad hoc,* have been set up by government for particular purposes. The U.S. Office of Education, for example, maintains an advisory committee on teacher exchange, consisting of representatives of such agencies as the National Education Association, the American Federation of Teachers, the American Association of School Administrators, and the American Council on Education.

Such official advisory bodies are valuable for securing sound counsel and for giving recognition to the contribution of private agencies and individuals to policy-making. They do not, however, meet the entire need. Quasi-governmental agencies are unable actually to coordinate voluntary efforts. Dependent upon government staffs, they are handicapped when it comes to advocating and building popular support for needed legislation. They may even find it difficult to criticize objectively programs in which governmental departments have a considerable stake. They are unable to take responsibility for actual operations by private agencies. Their relationships with agencies abroad are often limited to prescribed, traditional, official government channels. They are unable, because of their official character to undertake aggressive programs of education of the American public. They are likely to find it difficult to develop new, creative, experimental approaches to meet changing needs.

None of these limitations applies to wholly unofficial coordinating agencies. This advantage of voluntary organizations has usually been recognized by those government agencies involved in international cultural relations. They have accordingly welcomed the creation of strong private coordination machinery. The initiative of the American Council on Education, for instance, in establishing coordinating services to meet problems of educational reconstruction of war-devastated countries and the re-establishment of cultural relations with the occupied areas was encouraged by the State Department and other government agencies concerned. Another example of private initiative, partly in the interest of government objectives, was the development during World War II of the American Council of Voluntary Agencies for Foreign Service by joint action of the various major relief agencies working abroad. This council has cooperated closely with the official Advisory Committee on Voluntary Foreign Aid of the Department of State. With the end of the postwar relief emergency, both the council and the advisory committee have increasingly stressed educational and cultural relations, in addition to basic relief.

Other coordinating machinery has been supplied by operating agencies in specific cultural fields. For example, the Institute of International Education has long served as the focal point for coordination as well as operation of many forms of exchange-of-persons activity, particularly those involving academic institutions. The Governmental Affairs Institute, established initially as a panel of the COA, coordinates and administers the bringing of public officials and civil servants from abroad to the United States for advanced study. The National Social Welfare Assembly has performed a coordinating, as well as an operating, function in relation to international youth and community service projects and also sponsored the COA panel in these fields. The recently established United Nations Educational Service of the National Education Association coordinates the flow of information about international activities and programs of interest to teachers, schools, and educational institutions. The National Association of Foreign Student Advisers, a nonoperating group established by the Institute of International Education, provides informal coordination within its sphere.

Such nongovernmental coordinating agencies in the field of cultural relations are valuable to government in many ways. They can often tap sources of technical, professional, moral, and political support on behalf of some of our major national objectives. They can serve government agencies as advisers and as operators of specific projects. They can encourage needed legislation. They can provide useful professional criticism, when necessary, of government programs. But their principal function has remained that of assisting millions of individual Americans, through their organized groups, to find practical ways of participating directly in world affairs through tangible projects in international cultural relations. They have thereby often been able to direct private efforts into constructive channels, and to eliminate wasteful and dubious approaches.

THE VALUE OF COORDINATION
Implications of the Experience of COA and CIER

The value of coordination of voluntary effort is generally recognized, but its true meaning is commonly misunderstood. A dictionary definition of coordination is "harmonious adjustment or functioning." Too often the term takes on a far narrower connotation, sometimes even an unsavory one. This may have been the result, in part, of the extensive misuse of the term "coordination" during the Hitler period as the English equivalent of *Gleichschaltung,* meaning actually "political coordination" in the sense of coercing the individual to the will of the state, or even liquidating political opposition by force.

At its best, coordination does not imply either coercion, subordination of individuality, or discouragement of diversity. Coordination of American voluntary endeavor in international cultural relations has invariably implied dynamic, aggressive joint action to achieve international goals common to both private

agencies and to government. It has meant cooperative effort to
assist organized groups to develop sound, well-administered programs related to their own objectives and interests, in close collaboration with, but not subordinate to, government.

Coordination can achieve, through joint action, objectives beyond the reach of individual agencies. As the Gestaltists in the
field of psychology have reminded us, the whole is more than the
sum of its parts. Coordination as a dynamic action concept yields
returns superior to the total of individual uncoordinated efforts.
It can result in greater efficiency by each of those coordinated. It
can stimulate a greater total volume of sound effort by the combined agencies than that which the agencies working separately
can achieve. It can also build the machinery for those programs
which can best be conducted jointly. It can encourage diversity
while discouraging wasteful duplication.

The more passive "clearinghouse" concept of coordination also
has a place. This concept is, however, far more limited and, unless
supplemented by action approaches, may easily become stagnant.
Mere clearinghouse services have a tendency to remain at the level
of prosaic gathering and dissemination of facts. All international
efforts must, of course, start with the most complete and accurate
information obtainable and must provide for some interchange of
ideas. However, fact-finding and distribution alone rarely provides
a distinctive role for voluntary effort. This can often be done as
well, or better, by government. CIER and COA owed much of
their acceptance to their early stress upon the *action* implications
of the information they gathered. Facts about educational needs
of devastated and occupied areas were collected not as ends but
solely to stimulate sound effort. As one of CIER's members put
it, the commission was not a mere "clearinghouse," but was also a
"roundhouse," providing the lubrication which enabled its cooperating "locomotives" to run, and to start off on the track
directed toward their intended destinations.

It is, however, misleadingly easy to make a case for coordination in general. Like many other worthy concepts, it is not necessarily a good in itself. To be accepted by those to be coordinated, it

must meet actual felt needs. Needs are easier to discern in time of crisis. Both the private and governmental agencies concerned reached early agreement on the emergency goals to be achieved by CIER and COA. In these instances, the urgency of finding ways of stimulating sound group efforts, the need for establishing machinery for joint action, and the importance of a quick establishment of high standards of desirable voluntary effort were matters of common acceptance. Otherwise, resistance or apathy might well have undermined the work of both commissions and they could actually have been resented for disturbing the established ways of American organizations.

To be accepted and to be effective, coordination must be based, then, upon an urgent, fully recognized need for joint action to achieve tangible objectives. The emergency objectives with which CIER and COA dealt were reasonably tangible. It was at the same time an advantage and a source of difficulty that these objectives and needs were also temporary. When their purposes had been largely achieved, the commissions were disbanded, although somwhat later than originally intended.

Perhaps partly as a result of their emphasis upon education and upon the building of long-term relations, the termination of these two commissions resulted in demands by the participating agencies for continued and more permanent coordination under qualified educational leadership. Both the voluntary and the governmental agencies cooperating with COA requested establishment of supplementary machinery, adapted to more permanent objectives.

This demand for the extension of COA's activities by the creation of a permanent coordinating agency was expressed dramatically at the Second National Conference on the Occupied Areas in December 1950. The seven hundred delegates—representing more than two hundred voluntary organizations and the major governmental agencies involved, including persons who came to the conference from such distant points as Germany, Austria, and Japan—adopted unanimously the following resolution urgently requesting the American Council on Education to continue its leadership in the field of action coordinating service:

WHEREAS, An unprecedented number of delegates from voluntary agencies engaged in cultural relations projects in Austria, Germany, the Ryukyus, and Japan have by their presence manifested a firm determination to continue and expand these programs; and

WHEREAS, Officials of the Department of State and the Department of the Army have requested voluntary agencies (a) to undertake immediately additional projects to replace certain discontinued government operations in the cultural field, and (b) to assume responsibility for planning and executing long-range programs; and

WHEREAS, Both the governmental and voluntary agencies are now preparing to assume additional cultural responsibilities in Korea and other countries not named above; and

WHEREAS, Government officials and the representatives of voluntary agencies have demonstrated their deep appreciation of the services provided during recent years by the Commission on the Occupied Areas, and have expressed a strong sense of continuing need for a coordinating agency to identify cultural objectives and corresponding projects of greatest importance and value and to indicate ways and means of assimilating Austrian, German, Ryukyuan, Japanese, and other programs into broader international projects; therefore be it

1. *Resolved,* That the American Council on Education be requested to continue its leadership in this important field by maintaining an agency with the responsibility for stimulation and coordination of voluntary efforts in relation to Germany, Austria, the Ryukyus, Japan, Korea, and such other countries toward which both the government and voluntary agencies of the United States feel special cultural responsibility, and

2. *Be it further Resolved,* That the Department of State and Department of the Army as well as other federal agencies concerned be requested to give every possible assistance to the American Council on Education in this endeavor.

As a result of this demand, COA's Executive Committee submitted a proposal in February 1951 to the president and Executive Committee of the American Council on Education for the creation of a Commission on International Cultural Relations.[2] Similar resolutions were adopted at the various conferences of the American

---

[2] For the full text of the proposal see *An Experiment in International Cultural Relations* (Washington: American Council on Education, 1951), pp. 40–46.

Council on Education during 1951 and 1952. These are being studied by the Council with a view toward future implementation.

COORDINATION OF UNIVERSITY INTERNATIONAL PROGRAMS

The role of coordinated effort in reshaping university programs and services to meet new international needs has been the subject of particular study and discussion since the war. The vast potentiality of American higher education in world affairs has achieved growing recognition. But how this resource can best be tapped has been less clear.

Teaching and research in language, international relations, area study, and the related social sciences, are obvious contributions of universities to world affairs. A few direct action approaches, such as those involving interchange of academic personnel, have also been long established. But thoughtful educators are aware that this is not enough if higher education is to play an important part in international relations. By some leaders, nothing less than a comprehensive reappraisal of the total role of higher education in the light of new American world leadership has been demanded. Proposals have been made for a re-examination of the entire curriculum, of student guidance programs, of extracurricular activities, of research facilities, and of possibilities of direct services to the community, state, and nation relating to the growing world responsibilities of our people.

The many demands made upon the university during the war and especially during the immediate postwar reconstruction period have accentuated the process of self-examination. CIER and many of its cooperating agencies, such as the Institute of International Education, the World Student Service Fund, and the various associations of colleges and universities, early became keenly aware of the difficulties involved in translating existing university patterns, programs, and facilities, however well adapted to prewar purposes, to emerging international needs. This is reflected by the fact that virtually all of the major educational and professional associations included in their annual meetings between 1946 and 1949 discussion of their relationship to international educational reconstruction.

One of these discussions took place at the 1947 meeting of the Association of American Universities, at Iowa City, where the present author was asked to report on "American Universities and the Reconstruction of Higher Education Abroad." Noting some of the great contributions of American higher education toward healing the scars of war and re-establishing interrupted cultural contacts, he nevertheless pointed out several serious gaps and neglected opportunities for service. Recognizing that no mere administrative device could suffice to meet these needs, he nevertheless suggested that the major institutions consider the creation of all-university coordinating agencies for international relations, possibly taking the form of broadly representative "International Service Centers." For smaller institutions, strong, permanent action committees on international affairs were proposed. These centers and action committees would be designed to encourage re-examination of the total resources of the institution, locality, and service area for dealing with world affairs problems. They would also stimulate and coordinate international efforts. Among the scores of purposes which they might serve, the following specific possibilities were suggested:

1. To handle and improve selection, advisement, placement, and follow-up of foreign students and visiting professors.
2. To advise and place American students and faculty desiring foreign study, travel, and employment.
3. To promote sound student and faculty activity relating to international problems and interests—clubs, forums, lectures, exhibits, concerts, and the like.
4. To stimulate and assist the various subject departments to give appropriate international content and emphasis in regular courses.
5. To provide service and leadership to institutions, lay organizations, press, and radio in the state, community, or service areas through materials, advice, and a speakers bureau.
6. To develop a program of inquiry, research, and publication on international problems.
7. To serve as contact points between the college and international organizations such as the U.N. and UNESCO, and domestic organizations concerned with international affairs.

8. To serve as clearinghouses and referral centers for the increasing number of requests for information and aid received from abroad; and to formulate concrete projects to aid in meeting the worthiest of these and in carrying out various aspects of UNESCO's program, such as reconstruction, exchange of persons, fundamental education, and international understanding.

While special subsidization for such centers is doubtless necessary at the outset, many of their activities could be made income-producing,[3] particularly through special courses, lectures, publications, public performances, consultant services, and research under contract. Many universities, colleges, and communities have now taken some such step toward local reappraisal, coordination, and expansion of services.

Possibilities of strengthening university programs for international affairs were further enumerated two years later at a notable conference at Estes Park, Colorado, called in 1949 by the American Council on Education. There, under the theme "The Role of Colleges and Universities in International Understanding," two hundred representatives of institutions and organizations agreed that the time had come for a vastly expanded concept of the place of higher education in world affairs, and urged a simultaneous attack upon the problem through the creation of new coordinating machinery at both institutional and national levels.[4]

In the light of the Estes Park recommendations, a study was undertaken by the Carnegie Endowment for International Peace and the American Council on Education. This project, reported in *Universities and World Affairs,*[5] included a joint experiment in self-appraisal by eight universities. Beginning by testing certain hypotheses concerning the role of the university against actual current practices, it resulted in the development of a series of sug-

[3] See H. E. Snyder, "A Practical Approach to International Cultural Relations," *The Educational Record,* XXIX (October 1948), 369–70.
[4] Howard Lee Nostrand and Francis J. Brown (eds.), *The Role of Colleges and Universities in International Understanding* (Washington: American Council on Education, 1949).
[5] Howard E. Wilson, *Universities and World Affairs* (New York: Carnegie Endowment for International Peace, 1951).

gestions in the form of a check list of questions which institutions should ask themselves. These questions deal with basic hypotheses, international relations in the curriculum of general education, specialization training in international relations, international relations in professional and technical education, American studies abroad, extracurricular activities in international relations, off-campus education in international relations, research in international relations, and faculty participation in international relations.

Under the leadership of Howard E. Wilson, the Carnegie Endowment is conducting promising further studies along these lines in close cooperation with leading higher institutions. However, the various proposals for tapping more effectively the resources of American higher education have not as yet been implemented, despite considerable progress within particular universities and colleges. Instead of using their tremendous intellectual resources to blaze new trails for government policies and programs, and for voluntary efforts, most institutions and professional associations still tend to wait for their cue. They tend to undertake only what government specifically requests, to depend upon government contracts for services obviously a part of their regular responsibility in a day when world affairs dominate the lives of all. This academic lag has occasionally been referred to as social and moral escapism. Under pressure from government, and with government grants to institutions and students, vast expansion has been taking place in the natural sciences. While this expansion is doubtless necessary, it must be accompanied by corresponding acceleration of work in the social sciences, humanities, and human relations, by serious study of the total role and responsibility of the whole of higher education in a day of growing, and possibly permanent, international tension.

Despite the few promising developments cited elsewhere in this volume, progress in developing social institutions to cope with our new technical proficiency and capacity for self-destruction has seriously lagged. The university must share responsibility for this lag. Educational statesmanship is obviously needed as never before.

To marshal the resources and potentialities of American higher education for peace as they have been so successfully mobilized for the war effort, there is obvious need for carefully constructed co-ordinating machinery. Such coordination must, to be effective and to gain full acceptance, be more than an information service. It must reflect the dynamic conception of the role of coordination outlined above. It must be attached to a permanent, acknowledged voluntary professional agency, working in close cooperation with, but completely independent of, government. Such a coordinating service can assist each institution and organization to make its contribution to world affairs in ways adapted to its facilities and special interests, and to avoid the wasteful duplication of efforts which has often led to so much confusion and frustration in the past.

It is extremely doubtful, however, whether a major national coordinating service in international cultural relations should be established for higher education alone. Clearly universities have peculiar opportunities and responsibilities. But the world problems we are facing as a nation do not group themselves conveniently by educational levels. Meeting technical assistance problems or the needs of refugees, gaining better insights into the basic attitudes and aspirations of other peoples, establishing closer group-to-group relations between countries have little to do with educational levels as we know them in the United States. To set up one coordinating service for higher education and another for elementary and secondary education, and still another for nonacademic relations can be wasteful and confusing. The approach employed by COA and CIER as outlined above avoids such duplication and artificial stratification.

5.

Neglected Aspects of
International Cultural Relations

IT IS FAR EASIER to make the case for international cultural relations than to build sound programs. The limitless opportunities in the cultural relations approach are likely to obscure the numerous pitfalls which beset the path of those attempting to apply it. Some of these pitfalls derive from our present ignorance of fundamentals—of the values men hold, of basic sources of human conflict, of how peoples learn to work together, of areas of fruitful interchange, of ways of appraising results, of the appropriate role of government and of private endeavor. Neglect of such fundamentals can cause needless frustration, and even, in extreme cases, actual ill-will where understanding is the object. Mutually satisfying relationships among peoples do not result automatically from mere contact, but must be consciously promoted, carefully nurtured, and constantly evaluated.

The discussion of neglected aspects of international cultural relations, which follows, is intended partially as a summary of some of the principal points brought out in preceding chapters and as an introduction to later chapters, dealing with specific action possibilities. It is hoped that the many unsolved problems here presented will not be regarded as deterrents to action. They should rather be considered as challenges, as opportunities for urgently needed service in an area vital to the well-being of all.

1. *Clearer, more attainable objectives.*—This point should be too obvious to merit comment. Almost daily, however, new examples come to light of projects whose purposes have not been thought through, or which utilize methods clearly inconsistent

with stated objectives. Foreign guests studying the philosophy and techniques of American education may be whisked across several campuses a day. International conferences may underestimate the problem of communication caused by differences in languages. Official "good-will tours" abroad may have the opposite effect when planned without regard for what is appropriate and inappropriate to the particular national mores. When objectives of international projects are clearly defined at the outset and agreed upon by those concerned in each country, complete failure rarely results.

2. *Systematic evaluation of results.*—Despite the basic importance of evaluation, only a few systematic studies have been made, mainly of interchanges of persons. Organizations and institutions cooperating with such agencies as the Institute of International Education and the Commission on the Occupied Areas have been urged and aided to evaluate their own projects. However, only the merest beginning has been made, and adequate standards and techniques remain to be developed. Too many projects tend still to be based upon the optimistic assumption that interchange is good in itself, that such devices as study and travel abroad produce almost automatically good will and understanding. This assumption is easily refuted by citing (*a*) the tragic uses to which some of these exchanges in peacetime among European countries have been put in times of crisis, and (*b*) the impressions created by many Americans abroad.

Careful analysis of both immediate and long-term results of various types of cultural interchange is badly needed. Such evaluation should include field investigations, utilizing a variety of techniques including interviews, conferences, and studies of individual professional progress conducted some time after projects have been completed. Self-evaluation by sponsoring agencies during and immediately following projects is also important. Questionnaire studies and interviews and conferences just as projects are concluding can often be used to good advantage, but it is important to recognize their limitations in ascertaining why some approaches succeed and others fail. One of the major tests is the test of time.

3. Selection of appropriate devices.—Exchange of persons and international cultural relations are not synonymous, although commonly confused. The former is merely one of the major devices to achieve the latter. International cultural relations may take many other forms. Much work needs to be done to determine the appropriate role of each of the numerous devices which may be employed. Part II of this volume is devoted largely to a consideration of twenty-five "action approaches" to international cultural relations, but it was not possible to include all types of projects of great potentiality.

Better understanding of the possibilities and pitfalls inherent in these many forms of international cultural relations is needed. Attention should also be given to ways of combining several approaches to achieve better results. Agencies too often limit themselves unnecessarily in advance to a particular device.

4. Clarification of the appropriate role of governments, international agencies, and private organizations.—This need is brought out in the preceding chapters. The major categories of agencies sponsoring international cultural relations projects include: (*a*) United States government agencies, particularly the Department of State, (*b*) foreign governments, (*c*) intergovernmental agencies, particularly the United Nations and UNESCO, (*d*) United States voluntary agencies, (*e*) foreign voluntary agencies, (*f*) international nongovernmental agencies. Increasingly, projects involve various combinations of the above.

The question of determining the appropriate role of government and private efforts is partly a matter of resources and administrative competence, partly one of varying impact upon countries participating in projects. Government-sponsored projects may in certain areas, despite the best of humanitarian motives, be subject to the suspicion of political, or even of military, ends. Similar projects conducted by voluntary bodies or by international agencies may be relatively free from such suspicion. On the other hand, nongovernmental groups sometimes lack the prestige and the resources to gain the acceptance needed locally. A marked difference is apparent in the way in which different American voluntary agencies are received abroad. For example, in some areas where American missionary efforts or commercial activity is known, agencies associated in the public mind with such activities labor under a handicap, while in other areas such association could be advantageous.

The recent vast expansion in government international cultural relations activities into areas previously left to private effort makes it important to examine the impact of this changed sponsorship abroad. It is possible that some of the values of nonofficial direction can be retained by joint sponsorship of activities. In other cases, it may be found that initiative should be left to international agencies.

5. *Study of the impact of United States policies and programs abroad, particularly of attitudes engendered by cultural relations projects.*—This point is, of course, closely related to the one preceding, but seems sufficiently important for separate listing. It suggests far better analysis than is presently available of fundamental attitudes held toward the United States in other lands. Neither public opinion polls nor studies in cultural anthropology tell the whole story, valuable as they are. We need to know not only what people *say* they think about us when interviewed, but also what they are willing to *do* when the chips are down. We need to know how they react, and why, to our various national policies, to government economic and cultural programs, and to voluntary relief and cultural relations projects. To this end we need the knowledge and techniques of the social psychologist, political scientist, historian, cultural anthropologist, social worker, labor leader, agriculturalist, and specialist in mass communications.

6. *Efforts to reach the largest and most influential population segments abroad.*—In the past, interchange of persons and of ideas between the United States and other countries have tended to fall into six major categories of relationship: (*a*) diplomatic, (*b*) commercial, (*c*) technical, (*d*) academic, (*e*) tourist, and (*f*) missionary. Only relatively recently have attempts been made on a substantial scale, with the help of governments and foundations,

to bring about direct contacts between the largest population segments in our country and those abroad, namely agriculture and labor. This neglect has frequently resulted in distorted impressions of conditions and of political and social trends in other countries, to our serious detriment. Conversely, at least part of the misunderstanding of America abroad may be attributed to the lack of contact with a reasonable cross section of Americans.

The rapid transfer of political power in Europe, Asia, and throughout the world from the hands of the "educated" few and into the control of the laboring and agricultural masses directly affects Americans. We can no longer afford to remain out of touch with these groups. This suggests vastly increased stress upon non-academic relationships. It suggests further a varied program for the better interpretation here of the mind and status of the "common man" of all countries.

7. *Contact with "less popular" countries and peoples, rapidly assuming greater political importance.*—American cultural relations have overemphasized countries having close geographical, historic, or linguistic links with the United States. Even while starvation existed in Eastern and Central Europe and Asia, relief projects after the last war included substantial food drives for France, Britain, and Holland. Despite the greater language barrier and wider cultural gap, it is becoming a matter of political necessity, as it has long been a moral necessity, to develop closer cultural relations with the accessible parts of Eastern and Central Europe, Asia, Africa, and Latin America. An essential part of such an effort is the attempt to overcome the racial prejudice which inhibits our contact with, and reduces our influence in, most of these areas.

8. *Semantic clarification.*—Such terms as "international understanding," "exchange of persons," "world citizenship," "good will," and even "cultural relations" are used to convey varied and often contradictory meanings. They are in danger of becoming meaningless slogans. It would be useful to analyze the content of these concepts to determine, for example, the characteristics of the so-called "world citizen." There is particular need for finding

and stressing the *action* content of terms describing international understanding and cooperation. Does the person having a good intellectual grasp of world affairs qualify as possessing "world understanding," or is this reflected in his capacity for appropriate political and humanitarian action? Can we find terms which reflect more adequately the responsibilities of citizens in the modern world? Similarly, the term "exchange of persons," while based upon the sound principle of mutuality in international relations, is often used to describe activities which are not actually, and perhaps should not become, true exchanges. A far better term than "cultural relations" is also needed to avoid the "arty" or anthropological flavors here, and the *Kultur* implication abroad.

9. *Clearer insight into the relationship between domestic and international action.*—Both government and private agencies have encountered difficulty in recognizing this important new characteristic of our times. In this day of rapid mass communications, all peoples—Americans especially—live in glass houses. The way they keep house, the way members of the national family behave, is observed almost instantly by one's neighbors. Our *actions* now have far more effect than what we *say, think,* or *believe.*

Every sensitive American traveler abroad runs squarely up against this problem. His efforts at promoting good relations, and at interpreting American democracy, seem feeble indeed in contrast to almost daily stories in the foreign press and on radio about events in our country. Race and prison riots, bank robberies, gang murders, intemperate attacks from political opponents alleging subversion, scandals in government, demands by a prominent individual or two for preventive atomic warfare, purges of textbooks and teachers at the whim of pressure groups, denials of civil liberties, discriminatory immigration practices, and the like, tend to put Americans abroad very much on the defensive. Such reports are grist to the mill of those seeking to disparage Western democratic institutions and culture. We know that these manifestations are not typical, are excesses and abberations which have counterparts in most other societies. We know that the counterparts take even more vicious form in totalitarian societies. But to clever, anti-American propagandists no device is more effective than lifting directly from our press and republishing under the headline "Comment Unnecessary" such items as those mentioned above.

The essential fact is that we as a people can no longer afford the luxury, hitherto enjoyed as a result of our relatively isolated geographical location, of drawing a sharp distinction between the conduct or our domestic affairs and our foreign relations. For agencies interested in the promotion of sound international cultural relations, this means increased willingness to take a stand on domestic issues as well. It means that those who desire effective international relations can no longer avoid parallel action to strengthen and extend our own democratic institutions to eliminate those blots upon our democracy which undermine their work abroad.

For agencies which have hitherto considered their functions and their responsibilities to be exclusively domestic, it means a critical re-examination of both objectives and programs. Even cursory self-analysis is likely to reveal many points at which their effectiveness at home is at least partially dependent upon events in distant lands. Even their domestic purposes may best be served by concerning themselves with foreign policy, and with cordial relations with similar groups abroad.

10. *Better coordination of efforts.*—Discouragement and disillusionment resulting for duplicating, wasteful, ill-conceived projects could be documented in several volumes. To retain the advantage of wide participation by organized groups, institutions, and individuals, there needs to be a central, recognized, authoritative source of information, stimulation to purposeful effort, guidance, and coordination. Such an agency must be in close contact with needs and conditions abroad, with federal programs and policies, and with available operating agencies. This coordinating agency should not actually operate projects, because combining operations with policy-making and coordination tends inevitably to bias objectivity and to preoccupy the staff with day-to-day administrative routine at the expense of long-range planning.

In view of the growing tendency to develop international projects in terms of goals to be achieved rather than in terms of techniques readily available, a coordination service can be most effective if it is unlimited as to approaches with which it is concerned. Coordination of this type can no longer be effectively provided by agencies devoted to a single device, objective, or country. On the other hand, operating agencies can often function most effectively by concentrating upon and perfecting a particular cultural relations technique, by exemplifying a particular philosophy or religious viewpoint, by aiming at a single broad international objective, or by dealing with a limited geographical area. The role of coordination is to see that the best use is made of the resources of operating agencies, and that nonoperating groups of all kinds are encouraged and aided to develop worth-while, satisfying programs within their capacities and means. Other aspects of coordination are discussed in the preceding chapter.

11. *Achieving quicker results.*—Many of the points raised above suggest painstaking investigation over a period of years. The stress upon clarification of objectives, more precision in the use of terms, and improved evaluation must not be allowed to obscure the fact that we live in a time of growing tension and of unprecedented capacity for mutual mass annihilation. International cultural relations is inherently a long-term concept. It is essential that we find out which aspects of the concept are most productive of quick returns in building firm ties of friendship and understanding. Even while this is being explored, bold experimentation with seemingly promising new approaches must take precedence over slower "tried and found true" methods. This idea may be abhorrent to the type of academic mind which has often dominated international cultural programs in the past.

12. *Importance of national value systems.*—The significance of better understanding of the values which peoples hold has already been stressed in a preceding chapter. It is repeated here for emphasis. This point is closely related to the first on "Clearer, more attainable objectives," but has a slightly different twist. It actually belongs at the head of the list, since it is basic to all else. However,

it is, even for many people of good will, a somewhat difficult concept to grasp. For that reason it is placed last in the hope that earlier points may help to interpret it.

The goals, ideals, aspirations, and fears implicit in a people's culture largely determine the impact which cultural relations programs can have. This *Weltanschauung* is not easy for the outsider to discern, except as it comes to light in superficial, behavioral form. Even then, it is easy to overlook the fact that within national value systems individual and group values vary widely. Anthropology and the other sciences of human relations, with the assistance of religion and the metaphysical disciplines, should eventually point to some of the ways of discerning, defining, and interpreting value systems.

Most voluntary agencies working on international relations are unable to do much more than try to recognize this important factor. The very effort to explore it objectively may help them avoid unnecessary mistakes. If, in addition, such studies as those cited in chapter 1 can be applied to the problem at hand, planning will be on still sounder ground.

One element is often overlooked. The starting point in any study of comparative value systems is the better understanding of our own goals and values. This seems easy, but is actually most difficult to achieve. What do we stand for as a people? What are our basic objectives both at home and abroad? What do we most desire and most dread? Where do our values coincide with, and where do they conflict with, those of other peoples? How can we express our values so as to make ourselves intelligible and effective abroad? "Know thy God" and "Know thyself" are more than precepts. They are the cornerstones for all effective social action.

National value patterns often exhibit elements of considerable stability over the centuries. But they also change sometimes astonishingly rapidly. This is clear from a glance at the history of our own social and international objectives and standards of living of the past fifty years. It is therefore not enough to determine what the values of other peoples are, or have been. It is equally important to identify trends in value systems which may have a bearing upon the way international programs are related to emerging concepts at home and abroad.

Many of the types of projects described in Part II are already so designed as to deal with some of the neglected aspects just discussed. However, even excellent established programs may benefit from re-examination in the light of such factors as those cited in this chapter. As stated at the beginning, the suggestions above are definitely not to be viewed as deterrents to action. They must not weigh so heavily upon the reader as to make international cultural relations seem too difficult. Over-preoccupation with pitfalls and dangers can inhibit action. By far the greater danger lies in inertia, in waiting until all of the evidence is in, in approaching cultural relations projects with such diffidence that valuable time and golden opportunities are lost.

Despite the progress of science in human relations, trial and error learning will continue to be necessary in international relations, as in other fields. The aim of Part II is to encourage repeated trials, by helping to reduce the tribulations stemming from easily avoided errors.

PART II

*Making Action Programs
Effective*

6.

Criteria for Developing Voluntary Action Programs

How CAN our national association best contribute to international understanding? What can our university do to assist students and professors abroad? Can our local civic club assist children in war-devastated countries? What can our farm organization do to promote peace? Shall our school or college adopt a school abroad? Where are scientific books and good American literature needed? Shall we use our graduating class memorial fund to assist a work camp to offer a scholarship, or to send educational materials?

Questions such as these have poured in by the thousands since the end of World War II to the American Council on Education, the National Education Association, the U.S. National Commission for UNESCO, the Institute of International Education, and many other agencies. Much has been written about what to do, how to do it, and what to avoid doing. Scores of publications, hundreds of speeches, and thousands of letters have disseminated information. Why, then, are there not more well-planned and executed projects? Why have so many opportunities for constructive action been lost? Why does one encounter so many reports of frustration, irritating delays, misunderstanding, and even illwill?

International cultural relations and humanitarian endeavor of all kinds are always largely an "act of faith." But strong spiritual and philanthropic motivation does not preclude sound planning and administration. Voluntary international effort need not be hasty, impractical, slipshod. Voluntary programs can and often do meet high standards of careful planning and good administration.

The purpose of this chapter is to draw attention to some of the factors which every agency or institution should take into account before embarking upon international projects.

Each agency might begin by developing a list of criteria or standards to guide in the selection and conduct of international projects. These criteria should be suited to its own aims, interests, and facilities. The following check list suggests some of the major factors basic to virtually all cultural relations projects. The question form is used to suggest flexibility in their application, as the equivalent declarative statements run greater danger of being viewed as "absolutes."

Many of these factors are, of course, closely related. The comments under each are solely for purpose of illustration, and are not intended to be complete.

1. Objectives

What do we hope to accomplish by the proposed project? Does the project meet a real need? What immediate and long-range outcomes can be anticipated? How close are our objectives to those of other agencies active in this field? Can our objectives be understood and shared by cooperating agencies abroad?

> *Comment:* As an example, a primary objective of some cultural relations projects is to train technicians to meet urgent needs in their own countries. This purpose must be made clear to all involved in the project, especially to trainees themselves. If not clearly stated and frequently reiterated, such objectives can easily be sidetracked. Encouragement of foreign trainees to obtain university degrees of little use abroad may do violence to this objective. Since vague goals like "good will" may imply quite different things to different people, objectives must be sharpened in terms of concrete, attainable purposes.

2. Methods

What are the available techniques for achieving our objectives? Which methods are best adapted to our resources, personnel, and experience? What is the experience of similar groups employing these approaches? What research is available concerning the methods under consideration? Should a combination of techniques be employed?

Comment: Good relations can be damaged by insistence upon inappropriate devices. For example, in an emergency effort to raise food production in an area subject to famine, insistence upon starting with formal courses of study abroad may be obviously unsuitable. Field programs or demonstration centers may be more practicable ways to begin. Or, a combination of several methods—such as demonstration centers, technical missions, study abroad, and sending of books and equipment—may be necessary.

3. Use of operating agencies

Should the experience and facilities of operating agencies be utilized, or should independent administrative machinery be established? What are the pitfalls of independent administration of projects requiring technical skills, wide contacts, and considerable advance field investigation?

Comment: The operation of many types of cultural relations programs is far more complex than generally realized. For instance, affiliations with institutions abroad, interchange of books and educational materials, technical missions, work camps, and seminars involve extremely delicate and complicated processes of planning and administration. Trained professional workers are essential. Most national, and virtually all local, groups interested in such projects need, at some point, to work through established, qualified, operating agencies. If the maximum in educational and cultural relations values is to result, however, sponsoring agencies and operating agencies must so conduct their relations that the former, as well as the latter, remain in continuous, close contact with their own projects.

4. Relations with government

Does the project overlap, supplement, or complement similar government programs? To what extent is the advice and cooperation of government agencies needed? Should federal funds be sought?

Comment: Since government agencies and funds are now involved in many cultural relations activities formerly left to private initiative, voluntary efforts should be developed with full knowledge of related government programs. In many fields, supplementary private effort is essential since government-financed projects are more subject to misinterpretation abroad. However, it may be hard to justify or to arouse interest in substantial voluntary efforts in a country and in a field adequately provided for by large government programs, such as technical assistance or the Fulbright Act.

5. *Relations with other voluntary agencies*

How does the project relate to, and compare with, those of other agencies? Can it be so designed as to stimulate desirable activities by other agencies? Is there danger that it might deter needed action by others?

Comment: The educational value at home of international projects and their acceptance abroad depend in large measure upon the character, methods, and reputation of the sponsors, the operating agencies, and the cooperating agencies abroad. Widespread participation in the contribution of funds and efforts often offers a considerable psychological advantage. This advantage may easily be lost when other groups, however well motivated, enter fields of activity of established agencies. Those embarking upon new projects should therefore carefully appraise existing efforts and their relationship to them. It is particularly important that agencies dependent upon foundation grants, or upon a relatively small number of individual donors, select projects tending to increase rather than deter initiative by service agencies with a broad base of participation.

6. *Mutuality*

Does the project reflect a spirit of mutuality, of international relations as a two-way street? Does it clearly meet a need in both or all countries involved? Have safeguards been included to avoid the implication of "tutorial" or "Lady Bountiful" attitudes?

Comment: Assistance programs obviously cannot be conducted on the basis of a "one-for-one" exchange of goods, services, or personnel. However, planning and administration can avoid placing recipients in the role of "charity cases." Cultural relations projects, especially, can be so designed that the American sponsors gain fully as much as they give in knowledge, insight, and inspiration. Most projects, even those offering urgently needed assistance, can be so developed and conducted as to reflect the spirit of mutuality, of joint undertakings in meeting a common world problem. Each act by the sponsoring agency need not be matched by a reciprocal act from abroad. The factor of mutuality may be largely assured by joint planning involving both, or all, parties to each project, here and abroad.

7. Self-help

Will the project stimulate, or deter, initiative and self-help in the countries affected?

Comment: So-called "adoption" sometimes conveys the impression that rich American sponsors of an institution, community, or agency abroad will meet all the needs of the adoptee. Such expectations invariably prove erroneous and can cause much bitterness. The newer concept of "affiliation" tends to avoid this danger. UNRRA's famous slogan of "helping people help themselves" is equally valid for voluntary projects. Work camps and other jointly sponsored and executed projects are particularly designed to develop sound attitudes of self-help and independence.

8. Lasting values

Is the project so designed as to result in permanent, tangible gains, including lasting contacts and good will? Or is it likely to have only temporary value?

Comment: In general, concern for the development of lasting relationships distinguishes cultural projects from those aiming at short-term relief or meeting other immediate needs. This distinction can, however, easily be exaggerated. Even the distribution of food can be so handled as to provide for continuing friendly relations, and to serve as a point of departure for other forms of cultural relations.

9. Bilateral vs. multilateral action

Is the project inherently one for bilateral action, agencies in only two countries being involved, or should it be multilateral, involving agencies in several countries or working through an international organization?

Comment: Most international projects of American agencies are bilateral. However, strictly bilateral projects, involving an American agency working directly with a counterpart agency abroad, do not in all cases produce closer mutual cultural relations than those involving several countries. On the contrary, a bilateral approach may at times be a wasteful way of achieving an objective. It may even arouse suspicion of ulterior motives if it seems clearly within the scope and competence of agencies in other countries or of international agencies. Such activities as technical missions, seminars, and training for welfare services may often be made more acceptable and effective through joint participation of agencies in several countries. Even the objective of gaining friendship for the United States may, under particular circumstances, be best achieved by mutilateral or indirect approaches.

10. Evaluation

Does the plan provide for regular review and appraisal of results, both during and after the project? Should the appraisal include both self-evaluation and external appraisal?

Comment: Evaluation means objective appraisal of methods and results. At its best, it involves continuous reference back to primary objectives to determine how well they are being achieved. Thus, methods selected, and even the objectives themselves, can be modified promptly if found to be impracticable. Clearer and specific goals obviously lend themselves more readily to evaluation than do vague, general goals such as "good will."

Evaluation may take many forms. It should always, however, be continuous from the beginning of the project until long after its completion. Self-evaluation by the sponsoring agency is important. However, evaluation is more likely to be objective and valid when it includes critical, expert appraisal by persons not involved directly in the project. Increasingly, full-fledged research studies by competent social scientists are being employed by agencies eager to improve their international projects.

Among the most important elements in evaluation is the factor of time. Evaluative judgments derived during and immediately following projects, particularly when dependent largely upon reactions of sponsors and participants, are generally less valid than those secured after a reasonable time. Techniques employed during and just after a project, such as interviews, questionnaires, letters, and spontaneous expressions of gratitude may be important, but are rarely enough. The lasting values of projects can best be determined through delayed evaluation, utilizing not only the techniques just mentioned, but also, if possible, field interviewing and a study of actual progress toward achieving the goals of the project. On the other hand, too long a delay may make it difficult to secure data and to isolate the specific outcomes of a project from the impact of later experiences.

11. Follow-up

Does the plan provide for continued contact with the groups and individuals abroad? Are supplementary projects likely to be needed? Are cooperating agencies abroad sufficiently aware of the importance of follow-up and allowed to participate in planning for it?

Comment: Regardless of the degree of satisfaction which participants may feel during and directly after a project, enthusiasm wanes and contacts between individuals in different countries tend to diminish. Projects which include careful provision for specific, jointly planned follow-up activities are likely, everything being equal, to have more lasting value. For example, interchanges of persons sponsored by professional associations often include complimentary association memberships, free subscriptions to journals, placing individuals and organizations abroad on mailing lists, regular exchange of announcements of annual conferences and institutes, and encouragement of occasional contributions to professional journals by colleagues abroad. Such follow-up is more difficult with exchanges under government sponsorship. This is one of the advantages of joint government—voluntary agency sponsorship of projects dependent upon government funds.

12. *Information*

Should the project be widely publicized, or be largely "off-the-record"? What are the values, dangers, and best techniques for publicity? Should other interested private and government agencies be permitted to share the results? How can results best be disseminated?

Comment: Sponsoring agencies often overlook the possibilities of using the press, radio, and other media to publicize their projects. Human interest material based upon some international cultural efforts can desirably educate the general public to the importance of cultural relations. However, some projects have also been damaged by premature, excessive, or unwise publicity. Others have been harmed by failure to recognize that some public information techniques suitable in the United States are misunderstood abroad. Whatever the attitude toward general publicity, sponsoring agencies owe it to their own members and contributors, and to other agencies here and abroad, to share the results of their experience. Planning ahead for simple, direct, modest factual reporting should be part of every project.

The chapters which follow are intended to provide a few cues to agencies seeking practicable approaches to international cultural relations. They deal particularly with the nature, values, and limitations of the approaches most commonly employed. The statements are based largely upon: (1) the experience of the author in directing two major coordinating efforts in international cultural relations initiated by the American Council on Education between 1946 and 1951—the Commission for International Educational Reconstruction and the Commission on the Occupied Areas; and (2) the comments of a selected group of more than one hundred leaders in international relations in response to a special inquiry conducted during the early spring of 1952.

The material presented is neither exhaustive nor definitive. It should, however, suggest some of the major elements to be taken into account by agencies and institutions considering the various approaches listed.

It may be necessary to caution the reader also that the form of presentation employed is *not* intended to suggest that projects be limited to particular single techniques. On the contrary, it is often advisable to combine techniques to achieve a single objective. The *objective* must always take precedence over the *technique*. Serious errors in conducting international projects stem from excessive preoccupation with, or too early commitment to, particular devices. Scholarships, seminars, the provision of books and materials, and the rest are not ends in themselves. They are merely means of achieving broader goals.

The following chapters deal principally with approaches involving direct relationships between American institutions and agencies and those abroad. No attempt was made, due to limitations of time and space, to deal with many other valuable types of activities conducted solely within this country, however great their value in promoting international cultural relations. Such approaches as those designed to improve minority relations here, art exhibitions, special courses and institutes conducted in American institutions and communities, and other activities for the education of groups and individuals here are beyond the scope of the present volume. On the other hand, orientation courses and hospitality programs for foreign visitors have been included, since they bring Americans into direct personal contact with persons from abroad.

The chapters which follow draw attention not only to the services rendered by American agencies but also to values received by our organizations. Such values are largely educational, in the broadest sense of that term. Stress has, therefore, been placed upon those approaches which are of clear educational value to Americans, while at the same time of genuine service to other nationals.

7.

Interchange of Individuals

CULTURAL RELATIONS programs of the many types may be classified in several ways. For the purpose of this report they have been grouped into five categories: (1) those involving interchange of individuals; (2) interchange of groups; (3) interchange of materials; (4) affiliation between groups, educational institutions, and communities; and (5) projects of varying types not readily classifiable, such as those involving correspondence, American-supported institutions abroad, and interchange in fine arts.

Interchanges of individuals are among the oldest approaches to international cultural relations, and are doubtless the most extensive. During the academic year 1951-52, 31,000[1] foreign students studied in the United States. This represents a phenomenal growth from the approximately 7,000 reported in 1945. An estimated 20,000 American students studied abroad in 1951-52. But projects of interchange of individuals are not limited to students. During the past year, under government auspices alone, approximately 6,500 specialists in various fields came to the United States for advanced study, and an estimated 1,050 Americans were sent abroad for similar purposes. Professors, teachers, trainees of all levels, farm youth, high school students, representatives of labor, legislators, jurists, civil servants, and persons of all ages and occupations are coming increasingly to the United States for study, educational travel, and self-improvement.

This chapter deals with several of the major types of voluntary international efforts in which financial grants to individuals are involved. The programs here treated are designed primarily for

[1] *Unofficial Ambassadors* (New York: Committee on Friendly Relations Among Foreign Students, 1952), p. 14.

the advantage of *individual* participants. On the other hand, the group projects (treated in the next chapter) are either designed primarily for the advantage of organized groups, or are intended to enable a group to render a specific international service. Of course, many projects involve both individual and group interchange.

Programs of interchange of individuals, particularly those in which scholarships or fellowships are offered, generally stress organized study. Such study is usually for a period of one year, but may be for a longer or shorter period. Participation in special summer courses is common. In addition to formal academic study, an increasing number of projects include intensive individual study or planned observation for specific professional, technical, or other serious objectives. These nonacademic exchanges are generally of short duration, ranging from a few weeks to a few months.

In discussing each major type of project for interchange of individuals, the principal advantages ascribed to each, and their major limitations or pitfalls are listed. However, projects involving interchange of individuals are generally credited with several *common* advantages, and tend to share a few *typical* limitations, including the following:

Advantages commonly ascribed to interchanges of individuals:

1. The objectives of individual study and purposeful travel are relatively clear and definite, as compared with other categories of projects.
2. Programs can more easily be tailor-made to meet an individual's needs and interests.
3. The results of individual study are relatively easy to apply upon return home.
4. The results are easier to evaluate by following progress made by participating individuals.
5. Programs are often less expensive and easier to administer than group projects.
6. Individuals can readily be followed up, at least by means of personal correspondence.

7. Closely related to 6, programs are likely to develop lasting individual contacts.

Limitations commonly ascribed to interchanges of individuals:

1. Individuals can isolate themselves more easily than groups, sometimes at the expense of a sufficient range of contacts and experiences.
2. Individual planning of programs is more time-consuming for sponsors.
3. Younger visitors, particularly those remaining for a long time, may be "weaned" away from home countries, may be reluctant to return home, or may find readjustment at home difficult. Differences in standards of living may create difficulties.
4. Specialists are likely to devote considerable time to studying techniques which cannot be applied at home because of differing conditions.
5. Language difficulties tend to limit study abroad by individual Americans largely to English-, French-, German-, and Spanish-speaking countries.
6. Differences in educational patterns complicate academic interchanges and may result in misfits, either in age or academic level. Loss of time in the completion of educational programs at home is common.

As noted in the subsections which follow, interchanges of individuals are the subject of several intensive research and evaluative studies by such agencies as the Institute of International Education, the Social Science Research Council, the Woodrow Wilson School of Princeton University, the Hazen Foundation, and others. These studies should shed considerable light upon the factors which make for success or failure of interchanges of persons.

In this whole field, one single major voluntary operating organization is clearly pre-eminent, the Institute of International Education, although many others are active. For most government-financed programs the Educational Exchange Service of the International Information Administration, Department of State, assumes administrative or advisory responsibility. This office functions with the general policy guidance of the Advisory Commission on Educational Exchange, established by the Smith-Mundt Act. Agencies embarking upon new programs in this field should consult the Institute of International Education or the Department of State, or both.

The addresses of these agencies, and of the others mentioned in the chapter are to be found in the Appendix.

INTERCHANGE FOR COLLEGE AND UNIVERSITY STUDY

Purposes include:

1. To secure intensive academic or technical training in another country, either as an integral part of, or a supplement to, the student's educational program. Academic degrees may be sought, but often as a secondary objective.
2. To acquire or perfect another language.
3. To increase understanding of another country and culture through a relatively long-term experience in a particular institution or community.

Characteristics include:

1. Enrollment in an institution of higher learning for a year, or other academic unit of time, for graduate or undergraduate study, with some tendency, declining slightly in recent years, to favor the larger, internationally known institutions. Some projects limited to special summer courses.
2. Often scholarship or fellowship assistance through government grants, the Institute of International Education, a foundation, an institution, a national or local organization, or a combination of these.
3. Increasingly, orientation programs and special guidance by a faculty foreign student adviser on the staff, and special orientation courses for foreign students.

Advantages claimed include:

1. Involves a highly selected group of persons, relatively likely to assume positions of national and international leadership.

2. Language facility, receptivity to new ideas, and responsiveness to hospitality and individual friendship tend to be high for this age and ability group.
3. College and university setting provides a relatively natural environment, integrally a part of the culture of any country.
4. Usually provides a sufficiently long and intensive experience to eliminate erroneous national stereotypes.
5. Good facilities for guidance, general reading, and close personal contacts are available on most university campuses.

Factors sometimes overlooked:

1. Difficulty of adjustment to a different educational system. European university students, for example, are usually younger than American students but more advanced in such subjects as foreign languages, literature, philosophy, history, and the arts, while less well-trained in the social sciences. Advanced students are often disappointed in the limited offerings available in their fields of specialization.
2. Self-isolation of some foreign students, especially in larger institutions, causes them to miss social life, or to gravitate toward compatriots, so that they lose much of the value of study abroad.
3. Younger students who stay away from home for several years are sometimes reluctant to return, particularly to countries with lower living standards.
4. Foreign students in the United States, particularly those from Africa, Latin America, and Asia, find our pattern of race relations extremely difficult to cope with and to reconcile with our democratic political philosophy.

Research and evaluation:

The newly formed research and evaluation offices of the Institute of International Education and of the Educational Exchange Service, International Information Administration of the U.S. Department of State, are planning important studies. These will be reported from time to time in *The Bulletin* of the Institute of International Education, a monthly, and in *The Field Reporter,* formerly *The Record,* published bimonthly by the Department of State. The Social Science Research Council is also developing a program of research and evaluation relating to adjustment of foreign students, based upon intensive studies in three American universities coordinated with similar studies abroad.

The Hazen Foundation is sponsoring in 1952-53 a field study by John and Ruth Useem to evaluate study experiences of students from India for at least five years following their return to their own country. The Woodrow Wilson School of Public and International Affairs of Princeton University sponsored in 1950-51 an evaluation by O. W. Riegel of the effect of study abroad upon a group of Belgians.[2] Modest research projects have been undertaken by the National Association of Foreign Student Advisers, and by the Committee on Friendly Relations Among Foreign Students. The latter organization conducts, with the cooperation of the Institute of International Education, an annual census of foreign students in the United States, reported in its yearly publication *Unofficial Ambassadors.*

Agencies abroad sponsoring research and evaluative studies include UNESCO and the British Council. UNESCO publishes annually *Study Abroad,* listing such opportunities throughout the world.

Despite the increasing emphasis upon research and evaluation, there remains a serious dearth of authoritative knowledge concerning the factors making for successful and for unsatisfactory adjustment of students in countries other than their own, and of the long-term values and limitations of such study. The major philanthropic foundations are taking increasing cognizance of this need.

A partial list of agencies with operating or coordinating experience:

AMERICAN ASSOCIATION OF UNIVERSITY WOMEN
BELGIAN-AMERICAN EDUCATION FOUNDATION, INC.
CHINA INSTITUTE IN AMERICA

[2] For further summary see "Interchange for Advanced Professional Study and Research," p. 110.

CHURCH WORLD SERVICE
COMMITTEE ON AFRICAN STUDENTS IN NORTH AMERICA
COMMITTEE ON FRIENDLY RELATIONS AMONG FOREIGN STUDENTS
DEPARTMENT OF STATE, EDUCATIONAL EXCHANGE SERVICE, INTERNATIONAL INFORMATION ADMINISTRATION
FULBRIGHT ACT: Graduate Students
INSTITUTE OF INTERNATIONAL EDUCATION
NATIONAL ASSOCIATION OF FOREIGN STUDENT ADVISERS
NATIONAL CIO COMMUNITY SERVICE COMMITTEE
NATIONAL SOCIAL WELFARE ASSEMBLY
NATIONAL STUDENT ASSOCIATION
RHODES SCHOLARSHIP TRUST
ROTARY INTERNATIONAL (Harris Foundation)
U.S. NATIONAL COMMISSION FOR UNESCO (advisory)

INTERCHANGE FOR SECONDARY SCHOOL STUDY

Purposes include:

1. To acquire a new language.
2. To increase understanding of another country and people through participation in school, home, and community life.
3. To utilize educational opportunities not available at home, especially when study is for long periods.

Characteristics include:

1. Age group usually between sixteen and eighteen.
2. Placement in a public or private secondary school, usually arranged by a national sponsoring agency.
3. Housing usually in carefully selected families or school dormitories.
4. Frequently, scholarship aid through a private agency, the participating school, and often with groups in the local community assisting.
5. Special orientation programs by sponsoring agencies and schools.

Advantages claimed include:

1. Can influence early the entire course of student's education and career.

2. Reaches younger students who are flexible and adaptable and acquire language and other skills readily.
3. Provides contact with basic social institutions of a nation—its home and community life, increasing the likelihood of sympathetic appreciation of another culture.
4. Is particularly well adapted to building international relations among farm and labor groups, university study being less common among these groups abroad.
5. Provides means of sensitizing families and entire communities to greater awareness of world affairs.

Factors sometimes overlooked:

1. Greater difficulty than with older students of adjustment to differences in educational pattern. The European concept of secondary education as primarily academic, pre-university study for the relatively small number of students preparing for the professions, contrasts sharply with the American concept of comprehensive universal secondary education. American high school students of the same age are likely to be considerably less advanced than European students in academic subjects.
2. Difficulty of adjustment to different family and community relationships, accentuated by emotional problems of adolescence.
3. Necessity of much closer supervision than for older students, with extreme care in selection and preparation of host families and sponsoring schools, and in finding suitable local leaders with sufficient interest and time.
4. Greater tendency than with older students to lose interest in home country, to try to extend stay unduly, or to encounter difficulties in readjustment upon return (may be obviated by extremely careful selection and orientation of students, or by using such exchange as an adjunct to school affiliations or other group relations projects).

Research and evaluation:

The American Field Service is undertaking to follow up children brought to the United States in 1948–49 by asking parents to appraise changes noticed. The American Friends Service Committee is studying student exchanges arranged between its affiliated schools. The Newton, Massachusetts, public school system has published a study of its experiences. Little authoritative research and evaluation available as yet.

Operating agencies and sources of information:

The American Field Service is virtually the only United States agency devoting its major attention to operating secondary school interchanges. However, farm organizations and national service clubs, and the Brethren Service Commission have also sponsored such interchange. With the assistance of the Office of the U.S. High Commissioner for Germany (HICOG), a substantial number of German secondary school students have been brought to the United States to study since 1949. Agencies able to provide useful information include those named below.

A partial list of agencies with operating or coordinating experience:

AMERICAN FIELD SERVICE
AMERICAN FRIENDS SERVICE COMMITTEE, SCHOOL AFFILIATION SERVICE
AMERICAN JUNIOR RED CROSS
BRETHREN SERVICE COMMISSION
DEPARTMENT OF STATE, EDUCATIONAL EXCHANGE SERVICE, INTERNATIONAL INFORMATION ADMINISTRATION
INSTITUTE OF INTERNATIONAL EDUCATION
NATIONAL CATHOLIC WELFARE CONFERENCE
NATIONAL EDUCATION ASSOCIATION
U.S. NATIONAL COMMISSION FOR UNESCO (advisory)
Many local school systems, such as that of Newton, Massachusetts

NONACADEMIC INTERCHANGE OF YOUNG PEOPLE

Purposes include:

1. To develop knowledge of another people by an early experience in common living, work, and recreation, not necessarily involving formal study.

2. To obtain broadening values of travel under particularly favorable, planned circumstances under sponsorship of organized groups.

Characteristics highly variable, but usually include:

1. Limited to summer vacations.
2. Travel, plus either living with families, work on farms, camping, or other outdoor living and recreation in host country.
3. Participants usually pay their own way, sometimes aided by sponsoring or cooperating organizations.
4. Guidance from cultural officers of embassies, ministries of education, schools, organizations, and local community leaders in selection and placement.

Advantages claimed include:

1. Has some of the same advantages as longer study, but, by utilizing vacations, avoids interference with regular educational programs.
2. Costs less, is easier to administer, and more flexible than many other types of projects.
3. Group projects of this type are more likely to provide contact with persons of several nationalities, in addition to hosts.
4. Provides motivation for study of languages, history, literature, international relations, etc., and often assists in language skills.
5. May influence vocational choices and social consciousness at a favorable age.
6. Is well adapted to build international contacts between agricultural and laboring groups.

Factors sometimes overlooked:

1. Participation usually limited to those who can afford it.
2. Necessarily more superficial than longer sojourns.
3. Because of brief contacts, more careful, intensive orientation is needed to avoid danger of misunderstandings and disregard of mores.

Research and evaluation:

Professor H. P. Smith of Bard College administered "before-and-after" attitude scales to 180 student participants in 1950 summer projects in Europe: 100 from the Experiment in International Living; 35 from the National Student Association; 20 from the Quaker International Voluntary Service; and 25 individual tourists. Thirty-seven Experimenters were also given standard interviews determining their feelings about countries visited.

The findings of the study will appear in a Harvard University doctoral thesis scheduled for completion in June 1953, under the guidance of Gordon W. Allport. Professor Smith's findings based upon the results of the attitude scales indicate that students as a whole did not become significantly more internationally minded or democratically minded or less ethnocentric, Fascist-minded, or conservative. He found a significant increase in gifts sent to Europe by all groups. The largest increase—100%—was by the Experimenters, doubtlessly attributable to the close ties developed with persons in the countries visited. N.S.A. students showed the next highest increase—30%—and a control group of stay-at-homes showed no increase at all.

Professor Smith suggests further evaluation of cultural relations programs by means of "before-and-after" studies, utilizing comparison groups remaining at home or participating in projects of different types.

The New York Herald Tribune High School Forum follows closely the careers and activities of returning participants, and keeps files on each individual. More significant evaluation is expected to be possible after fifteen or twenty years. At that time a survey will indicate what contributions former delegates are making in the area of international understanding.

A partial list of agencies with operating or coordinating experience:

AMERICAN FARM BUREAU FEDERATION

AMERICAN FRIENDS SERVICE COMMITTEE, QUAKER INTERNATIONAL VOLUNTARY SERVICE

AMERICAN YOUTH HOSTELS
EXPERIMENT IN INTERNATIONAL LIVING
INTERNATIONAL FARM YOUTH EXCHANGE
INTERNATIONAL FEDERATION OF AGRICULTURAL PRODUCERS
INTERNATIONAL WORK STUDENT EXCHANGE (inactive at present)
LOUIS AUGUST JONAS FOUNDATION, INC.
MENNONITE CENTRAL COMMITTEE
NATIONAL COUNCIL OF FARMER COOPERATIVES
NEW YORK HERALD TRIBUNE HIGH SCHOOL FORUM
WORLD STUDENT SERVICE FUND

INTERCHANGE OF PROFESSORS AND TEACHERS

Purposes include:

1. To provide, as an integral part of school and college programs, contact with another culture.
2. To secure the benefit of expert knowledge not readily available in an institution or country.
3. To establish cultural links between institutions and professional groups in different countries.

Characteristics include:

1. Assignments, usually for one year, assisted by U.S. Office of Education, ministries of education abroad, foundations, institutions, or by agencies administering the Fulbright Act (*see* Fulbright Act in Appendix).
2. In some instances, direct reciprocal exchanges of leaders or professors between two schools, school systems, or universities. This is especially true of faculty interchanges between public school systems.
3. Visiting teacherships or professorships, not necessarily actual exchanges, usually for an academic year, but may range from few weeks or a summer session to several years. Usually at the expense of the institution concerned, sometimes assisted by government and foundation grants.
4. Particularly common in modern languages and other typical academic studies. Increasingly applied now to other fields, especially those relating to economic, technical, and social services.

Advantages claimed include:

1. Acquisition of skills and knowledge not readily available at home.
2. Older visitors more likely to have a definite objective and to carry back usable knowledge.
3. When reciprocal, cost lower than for other interchanges.
4. Educators tend to be distributed somewhat more widely than students and other visitors throughout host countries, reaching smaller institutions and communities. Students tend to gravitate toward larger places and well-known institutions.
5. Educators particularly likely to disseminate widely their knowledge and experience in host country, and to spread at home what they acquire abroad.
6. Contacts and experience abroad by educators especially productive of lasting cultural ties.
7. Provides exceptional opportunity for objective mutual criticism of educational practice and philosophy.

Factors sometimes overlooked:

1. Language a greater obstacle in teacher interchange than for students or in other forms of interchange, since necessarily limited to those with exceptional language competence.
2. Wide existing differences in educational concepts, systems, levels, and methods. Also difficult to conduct interchange between countries of unlike culture, although such interchange is particularly needed.
3. Wide differences between countries in economic status of educators, making equitable salary arrangements difficult.
4. For some purposes, the relative inflexibility of persons of this age and professional group is a disadvantage.

Research and evaluation:

The study by O. W. Riegel, reported under the following section (see page 112), is also applicable to teaching interchanges. Modest evaluative studies are being conducted by U.S. Office of Education on elementary and secondary school teacher exchangees, and by the Institute of International Education, the Conference

Board of Associated Research Councils, and by particular institutions. Research studies which are either planned or under way by the Social Science Research Council and the Department of State may throw light upon this approach, as may the Hazen Foundation evaluation of exchanges with India.

A partial list of agencies with operating or coordinating experience:

AMERICAN COUNCIL ON EDUCATION, INTER-AMERICAN SCHOOLS SERVICE
AMERICAN FEDERATION OF TEACHERS
CARL SCHURZ FOUNDATION
CARNEGIE CORPORATION OF NEW YORK
CONFERENCE BOARD OF ASSOCIATED RESEARCH COUNCILS, COMMITTEE ON
    INTERNATIONAL EXCHANGE OF PERSONS
DEPARTMENT OF STATE:
    EDUCATIONAL EXCHANGE SERVICE, INTERNATIONAL INFORMATION
        ADMINISTRATION
    TECHNICAL COOPERATION ADMINISTRATION
INSTITUTE OF INTERNATIONAL EDUCATION
W. K. KELLOGG FOUNDATION
NATIONAL EDUCATION ASSOCIATION OF THE UNITED STATES
ROCKEFELLER FOUNDATION
UNITED STATES OFFICE OF EDUCATION
U.S. NATIONAL COMMISSION FOR UNESCO (advisory)

INTERCHANGE FOR ADVANCED PROFESSIONAL STUDY AND RESEARCH

Purposes include:

1. To provide intensive advanced or refresher training in their fields of specialization for mature specialists.
2. To add perspective and another dimension to study and research done in a single country.
3. To establish and strengthen international links between professional workers.

Characteristics include:

1. Generally, designed for persons having completed university study or other basic specialized training, and already recognized as specialists or leaders.

2. Participants older than student exchangees, usually aged twenty-five to thirty-five, or older.
3. May include enrollment in a university, but not necessarily.
4. Duration of study usually three months to one year, sometimes longer or shorter.
5. Nearly always facilitated by grants of funds from governments, foundations, or organizations.
6. Relatively little supervision as compared with student programs, but visitors are usually under guidance of a particular professor, or specialist, or professional organization.
7. Especially when government or foundation grants are involved, includes firm commitment to return to home country and continue service in field of study.

Advantages claimed include:

1. Relative ease of communication between experts in various disciplines.
2. Language often, although by no means invariably, already acquired.
3. Older visitors tend to have tangible, attainable purposes.
4. Results of study often immediate through publications and other concrete production.
5. Relative equality of status and scholarship of advanced students and researchers renders relations inherently reciprocal and mutual. Differences in educational systems, cultures, and philosophies are minimized for this group.
6. Convenient means of transmitting advanced knowledge where needed without implication of "tutorial" relationship. Especially well adapted to "refresher" training.
7. Less need for close supervision. Easy to individualize programs.

Factors sometimes overlooked:

1. Relative difficulty of mature persons in obtaining leaves of absence from their jobs and in leaving families, while excessively brief and superficial trips may leave erroneous impressions.
2. Heavy financial investment in or by each individual.

3. Many best qualified and most influential persons barred by past political activity or other visa, passport, and immigration barriers. Study abroad may occasionally be used as step toward emigration through marriage or other means.
4. Fully reciprocal exchanges are difficult, due to differences between countries in salary and living standards.
5. Sharp differences in technical development between some countries prevent adapting knowledge and best practice, and cause frustration upon return.

Research and evaluation:

Professor Oscar W. Riegel, director of the Lee Journalism Foundation, Washington and Lee University, conducted under the sponsorship of the Woodrow Wilson School of Public and International Affairs, Princeton University, an evaluation of exchange programs involving Belgians sojourning in the United States under the auspices of the Belgian-American Education Foundation, the Department of State, and the Rockefeller Foundation. Techniques to determine changes in attitude as a result of foreign experience include: (1) an attitude survey; (2) personal interviews; (3) interviews with group leaders to evaluate the political influence of former exchangees. Little significant change was found in the outlook of the exchangees after a period of time had elapsed. Riegel found, however, that the over-all feeling of exchangees toward the United States is one of warm, personal friendship, despite the fact that approval of our foreign policy does not always run high. Part of the study has been reported in an article for the French journal of public opinion research *Sondages,* and an article in preparation for *The Public Opinion Quarterly.* The Institute for Research in Human Relations conducted in 1951 "An Analysis of Attitude Change among German Exchangees." Efforts at evaluation are being made by many agencies including the American Association of University Women (requires two reports during study and one a year later); the National Council of Jewish Women; the Institute of International Education; the Social Science Research Council; the National Social Welfare Assembly;

the Conference Board of Associated Research Councils; the Governmental Affairs Institute; the Department of State, International Information Administration and UNESCO Relations Staff; the British Council; and the American National Red Cross.

A *partial list of agencies with operating or coordinating experience:*

AMERICAN ASSOCIATION OF UNIVERSITY WOMEN
AMERICAN CHEMICAL SOCIETY
AMERICAN HOME ECONOMICS ASSOCIATION
AMERICAN NATIONAL RED CROSS
AMERICAN-SCANDINAVIAN FOUNDATION
BELGIAN-AMERICAN EDUCATION FOUNDATION, INC.
CARNEGIE CORPORATION OF NEW YORK
COMMONWEALTH FUND
CONFERENCE BOARD OF ASSOCIATED RESEARCH COUNCILS, COMMITTEE ON
    INTERNATIONAL EXCHANGE OF PERSONS
DEPARTMENT OF STATE:
    EDUCATIONAL EXCHANGE SERVICE, INTERNATIONAL INFORMATION
        ADMINISTRATION
    TECHNICAL COOPERATION ADMINISTRATION
GOVERNMENTAL AFFAIRS INSTITUTE, INC.
INSTITUTE OF INTERNATIONAL EDUCATION
LEAGUE OF WOMEN VOTERS
NATIONAL CATHOLIC EDUCATIONAL ASSOCIATION
NATIONAL CONFERENCE OF CHRISTIANS AND JEWS
NATIONAL COUNCIL OF JEWISH WOMEN
NATIONAL SOCIAL WELFARE ASSEMBLY
ROCKEFELLER FOUNDATION
SOCIAL SCIENCE RESEARCH COUNCIL
U.S. NATIONAL COMMISSION FOR UNESCO (advisory)

8.

Interchange of Groups

INCREASINGLY, individuals desiring to study or travel abroad are seeking such experience in organized groups. Seminars, work camps, youth exchanges, conferences, missions, international centers, and group travel involve tens of thousands of persons annually.

Group interchange tends to differ from interchange of individuals in its central objective, the former being designed primarily for the advantage of a *group,* or for rendering a specific service requiring *joint action* by a number of individuals. Group interchange tends also to be for shorter periods of time than that of individuals, usually utilizing summer vacations. It is generally sponsored by a national or international agency, although sometimes local groups or institutions serve as sponsors.

Those conducting, or conversant with, interchange of groups for international cultural relations ascribe to them the following distinctive advantages and limitations:

Advantages commonly ascribed to group projects:

1. Individuals are more likely to be, and to remain, motivated by the service objective of a group they are part of, than by individual purposes.
2. *Esprit de corps* is easier to develop and maintain than the morale of individuals working independently.
3. An experience shared is more easily interpreted, evaluated, and followed up.
4. Arrangements can more readily be made to secure a wide range of contacts and experiences for a group than for individuals.

5. Group activity is more likely to be related to the work of continuing agencies, and therefore to be of lasting value.
6. Limitations of individuals, such as lack of language or other skills, are likely to be compensated for by others in the group.
7. Travel and other arrangements tend to be less expensive per capita.

Limitations commonly ascribed to group projects:

1. Much depends upon selection of leaders and participants. A few wrong choices can damage the experience of an entire group.
2. Skilled planning by a qualified agency with wide field experience is essential and too often lacking.
3. Even with careful planning, it is difficult to find projects which meet real needs of, or experiences which are of value to, all members of the group.
4. Available time is usually very limited. The tendency is to try to do too much.

In contrast to interchanges of individuals no coordinating agencies are capable of offering adequate guidance on group projects of all or most major types. For relief and other assistance projects, the American Council of Voluntary Agencies for Foreign Service has been providing guidance and coordination since early in World War II. For cultural reconstruction, and projects involving occupied Germany, Japan, Austria, and the Ryukyus, the American Council on Education provided active leadership between 1946 and 1951 through sponsorship of two coordinating commissions, but is at present inactive. For organized educational travel, the Council on Student Travel has exercised leadership since 1945. For seminars, work camps, and international centers the American Friends Service Committee is one of several principal operating agencies. A valuable central source of information about group projects of many types is the U.S. National Commission for UNESCO. The addresses of the above agencies, and those mentioned under types of projects may be found in the Appendix.

INTERNATIONAL SEMINARS

Purposes include:

1. To provide by means of a short, intensive educational experience, usually during vacation, improved understanding of international issues; to perfect a language; or to provide advanced training in a special field.
2. To obtain the advantages of group experience through bringing together a relatively homogeneous group.
3. To combine study, discussion, and recreation as a means toward building mutual understanding and friendship.

Characteristics include:

1. Time range from less than three weeks to two months.
2. Sponsorship by service agencies, educational institutions, international agencies, and professional organizations.
3. Participants usually university students or specialists in a particular field, representing several nationalities.
4. Costs usually met fully or partially by participants; scholarships sometimes available.
5. Stress on group living and recreation, as well as serious study.
6. Program usually highly informal, stressing discussion rather than lectures.
7. Emphasis generally upon a specific field of interest, but program frequently flexible, with entire group sharing planning responsibility.
8. Leadership provided by directors, teams, or chairmen, supplemented by specialists available for all or part of the time.
9. Results generally summarized in written report.

Advantages claimed include:

1. Sufficiently intensive experience to leave lasting impressions and to form lasting personal friendships.
2. Well adapted to informal give-and-take between leaders and participants and among latter, the presence of experienced leaders keeping discussions focused and preventing them from

becoming too emotional or from reaching controversial impasses.

3. Utilizes largest block of time available to most participants without interruption of a year's work or study. Can supplement desirably courses and other intellectual experiences.
4. May offer opportunity for additional language training.
5. Often provides techniques of communication as well as professional training usable in home country.
6. Provides thorough familiarity with a small area, a community, or an institution and, through exchange of experiences and opinions, provides a broad knowledge of the host country.
7. May result, when the participants are specialists, in concrete proposals and programs capable of being implemented at once, especially when all major nationalities and interests concerned are present.

Factors sometimes overlooked:

1. Scarcity of expert leadership and expense involved in employing highly trained personnel.
2. Difficulties in reconciling differing age groups, educational levels and concepts, and social and political outlooks.
3. Language barrier, especially for those unable to use their own language at the seminar.
4. Tendency in student seminars occasionally to form nationality cliques, or for men and women to "pair off," interfering with group spirit.
5. Highly informal technique generally employed sometimes difficult to reconcile with high intellectual level and seriousness of problems presented.

Research and evaluation:

No actual research available, but most sponsors attempt informal evaluation. The Salzburg Seminar, the M.I.T. International Student Project, UNESCO, and the American Friends Service Committee, all stress evaluation throughout and after a seminar, depending mainly upon interviews, group discussions, reports from leaders, and correspondence.

A partial list of agencies with operating
or coordinating experience:

AMERICAN FRIENDS SERVICE COMMITTEE
INSTITUTE OF INTERNATIONAL EDUCATION
MASSACHUSETTS INSTITUTE OF TECHNOLOGY, INTERNATIONAL STUDENT
  PROJECT
SALZBURG SEMINAR IN AMERICAN STUDIES
U.S. NATIONAL COMMISSION FOR UNESCO (advisory)

WORK CAMPS
International Service Projects

Purposes include:

1. "To build peace through small international groups of volunteers, working, living and learning together" (motto of international work camp movement).
2. To render needed services to a community as a means to
   mutual understanding.
3. To provide intensive contact with a small, but typical, segment
   of a foreign culture.

Characteristics include:

1. International teams of approximately fifteen to twenty-five
   young men and women, including nationals of host country,
   undertaking to meet a real need of a community in a distressed
   area.
2. Length of service ranging from two weeks to one year, generally
   five or six weeks during the summer.
3. Projects sponsored by national or international voluntary organizations, often affiliated with religious groups.
4. Trained leaders sometimes paid, or received dependency allow-
   ances, but participants come at their own expense, including
   cost of transportation, unless scholarship aid available.

5. Work with hands at least half of each day, simple cooperative living, group recreation, combined with discussion of social and international problems.
6. Projects planned in close cooperation with community and country. Great care exerted to avoid competition with local paid labor.
7. Volunteers for projects abroad selected generally after similar experience in their own country; most frequently students and teachers, but increasingly also persons of other occupations; usually of varied religious and racial backgrounds.

Advantages claimed include:

1. Learning by doing and by rendering service, rather than by mere talking or receiving instruction.
2. Satisfaction of manual labor, combined with intellectual stimulation, fellowship, experience in cooperative living, and interaction with members of another society.
3. Opportunity to learn to understand a specific place or region, its problems, customs, and people.
4. Well adapted to bring together persons of diverse social, educational, and occupational backgrounds.
5. Learning process largely spontaneous and unself-conscious.
6. Demonstration of clearly humanitarian international action.

Factors sometimes overlooked:

1. Difficult to overcome attitudes of some nationalities and social groups toward manual labor and primitive living.
2. Hard to select projects meeting definite, recognized, community needs and providing meaningful work, and to interpret needs accurately to work-campers.
3. Extreme care in selection essential, with emphasis usually upon mature individuals of varied religious and racial background, preferably experienced in similar projects at home and dedicated in advance to making project totally effective. Problem of selection includes weeding out those seeking cheap travel or who are emotionally unfit.

4. Leadership is crucial, but it is difficult to obtain persons with requisite knowledge of democratic processes and ability to apply these in unusual group situation. Administrative competence, teaching ability, international outlook, technical skills, and skill in interpreting foreign cultures, are desirable.

Research and evaluation:

Henry W. Riecken, of Harvard University, has completed a psychological evaluation of American Friends Service Committee work camps in the United States and Mexico. His study focuses on the changes in attitudes and personality characteristics resulting from work camp participation, and is scheduled for publication late in 1952 by the Addison-Wesley Press, Cambridge, Mass., under the title "The Volunteer Work Camp: A Psychological Evaluation." The book will contain an Appendix written by Gordon W. Allport, summarizing his evaluation of the AFSC work camp program in Europe in 1948.

Riecken administered questionnaires to the 1948 work-campers before, immediately after, and nine months after participation. He found that participants became significantly more altruistic, less prejudiced, more democratic, and less authoritarian—remaining so after a year. They became more critical of the traits they associate with the "average American." Campers became less aggressive, but more independent; less anxious about success, but more ambitious for achievement. They increased in self-reliance, self-confidence, and self-direction. Work camp changed the vocational plans of about one-quarter of the campers toward "service-oriented" occupations. A smaller proportion who had chosen such occupations before attending camps changed their minds afterward. The most enduring effects were on campers having continued contact with one another after returning home.

Several other studies are under way, including those of Howard P. Smith of Bard College (mentioned under nonacademic youth projects, page 107), and Olle Vejde, secretary of the Association of International Work Camps for Peace. The American Friends Service Committee and other agencies are increasingly stressing both self-evaluation and external evaluation by educators and social scientists.

A partial list of agencies with operating or coordinating experience:

American Friends Service Committee, Quaker International Voluntary Service

Association of International Work Camps for Peace (coordinating)

Brethren Service Commission

Christian Work Camps Fellowship of Canada

Congregational Christian Service Commission

Coordinating Committee for International Voluntary Work Camps (coordinating)

International Youth Hostels Federation

Mennonite Central Committee, Inc., Mennonite Voluntary Service

Methodist Student Service

Service Civil International

United Christian Youth Movement, Youth Service Projects, U.S.A., (coordinating)

Universalist Service Committee

World Alliance of Young Men's Christian Associations

World Council of Churches

World Union of Jewish Students

World University Service

CONFERENCES, INSTITUTES, AND WORKSHOPS

Purposes include:

1. To combine exchange of information, ideas, and intellectual stimulation among persons of similar professional or academic background, with effort to find solutions to particular problems of international significance.
2. To exchange specific technical knowledge and skills.
3. To provide an experience in democratic planning and in universal participation, all members of the group working together on a common problem.

Characteristics include:

1. Usually sponsored by international organizations or national organizations with international programs, also occasionally by an institution.
2. Usually for about twenty-five to fifty mature persons of similar professional background, but may be adapted to many purposes, types of participants, and groups of varying size.
3. Often aimed at solution of a particular problem of concern to a selected, fairly homogeneous group of participants.
4. Participants generally chosen by invitation or by reason of membership in an organization or professional group.
5. Highly informal in organization, utilizing modern discussion techniques, committees or working parties, and group recreation. Relatively little use of lectures and formal presentations. Participants often assist in program planning.
6. Usually includes an attempt at self-evaluation, involving leaders and participants, with occasional effort at objective, external appraisal.
7. Usually results in a substantial report of findings concerning the topic of the conference, the conference process itself, and the techniques employed.
8. Approach closely related to that of seminars, but usually designed for a somewhat older group, with less academic emphasis, and conducted somewhat more informally. May closely resemble informal seminars.

Advantages claimed include:

1. Better adapted than more formal advanced study or than seminars to a free interchange of ideas, and to solving of a specific common problem.
2. By combining joint recreation with work and discussion, facilitates formation of close personal friendships, and reduces somewhat language and other cultural barriers.
3. Provides an example of "democracy in action," through free give-and-take, and relatively equal status of staff and partici-

pants. Chairman leads, but does not dominate, endeavoring to bring out contributions of each participant.

4. Good setting for overcoming defensive reactions of certain individuals and national groups by concentrating upon a problem common to all.
5. Relatively easy to combine careful self-evaluation with this technique, and to follow up results.

Factors sometimes overlooked:

1. Difficulty in providing skilled leadership.
2. Necessity of careful advance planning and interpretation of informal methods to avoid impression that purposes are vague and methods slipshod.
3. Language obstacle may seriously handicap otherwise qualified participants.
4. Tendency of some nationalities to want to give or hear lectures.
5. Desire to cover too much ground.

Research and evaluation:

Objective external analysis is rare, although almost all projects stress self-evaluation. Such evaluation may take several forms—a session or two at the end, an evaluation committee meeting throughout, or planned follow-up by correspondence of later reactions of participants. When the topics or problems are directed at action approaches or specific solutions, evaluation is partially inherent in the actual results achieved. These can then be checked periodically to determine whether ultimate goals are being reached.

A significant attempt at evaluation of a small international conference is to be found in a forthcoming doctoral dissertation of Mrs. Jacqueline Sutton of the Department of Social Relations, Harvard University, entitled "A Case History of an International Conference." Based upon a UNESCO conference of social scientists held in 1948 to discuss "Factors Making for National Aggressiveness and International Understanding," the study concentrated upon "barriers to communication" based upon contrasting ideologies of participants and upon the formation of cliques during this conference. The study includes an analysis of the nature of the barriers, their types, the reasons for the success of the conference, and the interaction process.

The summer Bethel, Maine, National Training Laboratory in Group Relations has conducted several significant experiments on domestic phases of this technique. The Lisle Fellowship, working primarily with students and younger people, particularly stresses evaluation in its "human relations institutes." The Fellowship's program has also been objectively evaluated in various studies, including two by Dr. Charles G. McCormick, one submitted in the Advanced School of Education of Teachers College, Columbia University, in 1945, entitled "The Reconstruction of Theological Seminary Education for the Preparation of Ministers for Religious Leadership in a Democracy," chapter 3; and a shorter study entitled "Creative Group Education in the Lisle Fellowship," written under the supervision of Professor Floyd S. Sampson, at the University of Denver, 1943. These reports may be obtained from the respective universities, or through the Fellowship. Mrs. Mary Jane McCormick's master's thesis at Massachusetts State College in 1942, "The Lisle Fellowship as a Method of Group Education for Democracy," and a master's thesis by Miss Amber Van at Teacher's College, Columbia University, also throw light upon the Fellowship's techniques.

A *partial list of agencies with operating or coordinating experience:*

AMERICAN FRIENDS SERVICE COMMITTEE
AMERICAN NATIONAL RED CROSS
LISLE FELLOWSHIP, INC.
NATIONAL EDUCATION ASSOCIATION OF THE UNITED STATES
YOUNG WOMEN'S CHRISTIAN ASSOCIATION

Agencies studying the "group process" include:

HARVARD UNIVERSITY, DEPARTMENT OF SOCIAL RELATIONS
NATIONAL EDUCATION ASSOCIATION, DEPARTMENT OF ADULT EDUCATION
NATIONAL TRAINING LABORATORY IN GROUP RELATIONS, BETHEL, MAINE

University of Michigan, Group Relations Laboratory
World Federation for Mental Health (advisory)

Large International Meetings
*General Conferences, Conventions, Congresses,
Assemblies, Celebrations, Jamborees, etc.*

Purposes include:

1. To bring together for inspiration, information, and mutual stimulation a large number of persons of a particular international organization or with a common international interest.
2. To transact periodically the business of an international organization, usually permitting widespread membership participation in its affairs.
3. To commemorate a particular historical event or a prominent person.
4. To obtain favorable publicity for a particular program, agency, or social objective, and to strengthen popular support therefor.

Characteristics too varied to enumerate, but may include:

1. Regular conferences of international organizations, usually held annually or biennially, sometimes less frequently. Attendance by official delegates, but sometimes open to all members and to other interested persons.
2. In case of special congresses, assemblies, or jamborees of organized voluntary groups, usually called by an international organization or group of organizations working together.
3. Special celebrations, conferences, and congresses, sometimes initiated by government agencies of a particular country, or by religious societies, especially when purpose is commemorative of a person or event.
4. Attendance varies from less than a hundred to many thousands.
5. Emphasis on lectures, concerts, performances, or other formal presentations, often supplemented by smaller conference discussions and working parties.
6. Formal statement of findings and resolutions, especially in cases where purpose is promotion of an international social objective.

Advantages claimed include:

1. Permits widespread individual participation in international programs.
2. Convenient way of disseminating information widely, and stimulating desired action.
3. Means of attracting prominent public figures.
4. Opportunity for publicity, ceremonies, and pageantry with attendant stimulation of members and general public, and spreading of objectives.
5. Easier to arrange less frequent large meetings than several small ones.
6. More representative and usually more broadly international than smaller gatherings sponsored by large organizations and groups.
7. Usually includes exhibits and special cultural events not possible at smaller meetings.

Factors sometimes overlooked:

1. Difficulty involved in integrating nationalities, especially at large meetings, national delegations tending to stick together.
2. Lack of opportunity for individual participation because methods are necessarily more formal.
3. Language barriers and resulting necessity of translation with consequent slowing of discussion. (Obviated to a considerable extent when simultaneous translation facilities are provided.)
4. Tendency of some large assemblies to overemphasize pageantry at expense of ideas.
5. Tendency of speakers to talk for the record.

Research and evaluation:

None available. Each sponsoring agency has its own approach to appraisal, usually combining subjective judgments with some statistics, particularly attendance figures.

Operating agencies and sources of information:

No central source of information exists. Sponsoring agencies are too numerous to list. UNESCO and the Union of International

Associations, Brussels, regularly list many of the major meetings in their publications. The Department of State also puts out an annual list of the international conferences in which the United States government participates.

Among the many international agencies with major affiliates in the United States holding large meetings at regular intervals are: the International Red Cross, the Boy Scouts, the Girl Scouts, the International Council of Nurses, Rotary International, the World Organization of the Teaching Profession, the World Federation for Mental Health, World Brotherhood, World Council of Churches, the numerous professional, religious, fraternal, labor, and civic and social welfare organizations.

ADVISORY AND CULTURAL MISSIONS

Purposes include:

1. To transmit quickly advanced technical information or skills needed in the solution of practical problems of a country or region.
2. To provide intensive opportunity for developing cordial fraternal relations between professional and other national leaders of two or more countries through sharing of experience and knowledge in relation to a particular issue or problem.

Characteristics include:

1. Participation often multi-professional, utilizing recognized experts in fields of greatest needs.
2. Usually depends upon volunteer service, based on leaves of absence from universities, agencies, or governments, with only expenses paid. Sometimes, especially when government and intergovernmental agencies owe individuals, honoraria are provided.
3. Projects developed at invitation of country visited and planned in close relationship to existing programs.
4. Varied methods employed, including lectures, demonstrations, discussions, conferences, refresher courses, and consultation service and visitation.

5. Often includes planned follow-up which may include correspondence, interchange of professional publications, sending equipment, invitations to conferences, etc.
6. Staff sometimes multinational, especially when under the aegis of UNESCO or other international agencies.
7. In some cases, when objective is primarily "good will," membership consists primarily of prominent figures in public life who speak and confer informally without endeavoring to transmit specific body of knowledge.

Advantages claimed include:

1. Short assignments permit recruitment of top-level personnel not available for longer periods.
2. Brings to country prominent personalities, new skills, and needed knowledge otherwise available only through publications or expensive study abroad.
3. May stimulate in both countries interest in interdisciplinary and international approaches and contacts. Stresses teamwork.
4. Meets actual needs by offering only those services requested.
5. Tends to be more dramatic and to get better publicity than long-term projects.
6. Since teams are involved, affords opportunity for checking impressions with others, and avoiding faulty generalizations.

Factors sometimes overlooked:

1. Risk of increasing superiority-inferiority attitudes, due to inherent donor-recipient relationship, though donors may also receive much in the way of cultural understanding and new knowledge.
2. Time sometimes lacking to study fully in advance needs of country visited and its ability to assimilate and apply technical knowledge. Danger of undertaking more than there is time to accomplish, because of superficial understanding of the problem, or excessively strenuous schedules constructed in response to eager demand for assistance.
3. Technically qualified persons sometimes turn out to be unsuited to international service.

4. Language barrier, which usually necessitates cumbersome translation, with attendant risks of misunderstanding and loss of time.

Research and evaluation:

Evaluation is being attempted by the Mutual Security Agency for its labor-management and other teams, but techniques are not as yet perfected. The Technical Cooperation Administration and the Department of State are also studying these techniques. The most important voluntary missions since the war have been those of the Unitarian Service Committee, which is studying ways of judging impact of its medical teaching missions over a period of time.

Not evaluative but indicating the range of such efforts is the Department of State's *Guide to Technical Assistance Services of the United States Voluntary Agencies Abroad,* prepared by the staff of the Advisory Committee on Voluntary Foreign Aid.

A partial list of agencies with operating or coordinating experience:

AMERICAN DENTAL ASSOCIATION
CARRIE CHAPMAN CATT FOUNDATION
DEPARTMENT OF STATE:
   ADVISORY COMMITTEE ON VOLUNTARY FOREIGN AID (advisory)
   TECHNICAL COOPERATION ADMINISTRATION
MUTUAL SECURITY AGENCY
TOWN MEETING OF THE AIR
UNITARIAN SERVICE COMMITTEE
U.S. NATIONAL COMMISSION FOR UNESCO (advisory)

TECHNICAL ASSISTANCE PROJECTS
Team Projects under Voluntary Agency Sponsorship

Purposes include:

1. To assist a country in raising living standards through provision of needed technical aid, usually in fields of health, production of food and other basic commodities, housing, welfare, and education.

2. To provide through private effort forms of assistance less well-adapted to bilateral or multilateral government action, with a particular stress upon human relations values.
3. To provide demonstrations of best practice and technique of cooperation in meeting needs of particular communities.

Characteristics include:

1. Usually involves teams of five to twenty persons of varied specialties working jointly with persons of a particular country or community to meet a pressing local problem.
2. Staff usually, but not necessarily, recruited from a single country.
3. Generally lasts one to two years, but sometimes longer, or may be limited to a single summer. Summer and short-term projects are often auxiliary to longer-term programs and may involve younger people and resemble work camps.
4. Organized upon invitation of country and community involved, and developed in close collaboration with governmental or intergovernmental agencies.
5. May be privately financed, but usually government of country assisted shares in cost. Sometimes financed wholly or partially by contracts with government or intergovernmental agencies. Indigenous voluntary agencies often share cost.
6. Stresses community cooperation, human relations, and spiritual values along with technical assistance.
7. Generally involves work in so-called underdeveloped areas of Asia, Africa, and Latin America, but some sent also to Europe.
8. At best, includes substantial orientation and training program, including language training.

Advantages claimed include:

1. Easier for voluntary technical assistance to establish humanitarian objectives in minds of recipients, and to overcome suspicion of political or ulterior motives than in case of official projects.
2. Government and intergovernmental programs tend to stress

official relationships and expert-to-expert relations, while voluntary projects stress contact with the common people of the country or community and emphasize noneconomic values.

3. Technical demonstrations and experimentation sometimes more easily carried on by private agencies and may later be taken over by official agencies.
4. Team approach permits building group morale, while providing range of needed skills.
5. Length of assignment makes it practicable to prepare personnel in languages, area study, etc., permitting relatively lasting contribution.
6. Voluntary agency personnel, especially those of religious service organizations, may be less likely to be discouraged by difficult conditions encountered, may better reflect spirit of cooperation, and may more readily promote long-term cultural ties between groups in both countries.
7. Area, language, and technical experience acquired by staffs may later be valuable in government and United Nations projects.

Factors sometimes overlooked:

1. Danger of assuming easy solutions to problems with roots deep in cultural and economic organization; may be harder than for official agencies to arrange for authoritative advance analysis of needs.
2. Expensive type of voluntary effort. Often more difficult for private agencies to employ technically qualified persons and expert administrators.
3. Some agencies, especially sectarian religious groups, may encounter local misunderstanding of motives.
4. Difficult to develop attitudes of mutuality and self-help, for, as in other assistance projects, donor-recipient relationship is inherent. Values *received* may be harder to discern than those *contributed*.
5. Assistance withdrawn, or conducted without plan for follow-up, may produce frustration and ill will.

Research and evaluation:

Much informal evaluation and research, largely under government and United Nations auspices, including the Department of Agriculture, the Technical Cooperation Administration of the Department of State, the Mutual Security Agency, the Technical Assistance Administration of the U.N., and UNESCO. Increasingly, foundations and private operating agencies, such as the American Friends Service Committee and the Near East Foundation are concerning themselves with objective analysis of outcomes.

The Public Affairs Institute, Washington, D.C., has published a series of pamphlets on technical assistance of interest to voluntary agencies. The *Guide to Technical Assistance Services of United States Voluntary Agencies Abroad,* mentioned in the preceding section, also gives such information.

A partial list of agencies with operating or coordinating experience:

AMERICAN COUNCIL OF VOLUNTARY AGENCIES FOR FOREIGN SERVICE (advisory)

AMERICAN FRIENDS SERVICE COMMITTEE

BRETHREN SERVICE COMMISSION

DEPARTMENT OF AGRICULTURE, OFFICE OF FOREIGN AGRICULTURAL RELATIONS

DEPARTMENT OF STATE:

ADVISORY COMMITTEE ON VOLUNTARY FOREIGN AID (advisory)

TECHNICAL COOPERATION ADMINISTRATION

INTERNATIONAL BASIC ECONOMY CORPORATION

MUTUAL SECURITY AGENCY

NEAR EAST FOUNDATION

U.S. NATIONAL COMMISSION FOR UNESCO

Intergovernmental operating agencies include:

TECHNICAL ASSISTANCE ADMINISTRATION OF THE UNITED NATIONS, including cooperating specialized agencies, especially FOOD AND AGRICULTURE ORGANIZATION, INTERNATIONAL LABOR OFFICE, WORLD HEALTH ORGANIZATION, and UNESCO

INTERNATIONAL CENTERS

Purposes include:

1. To provide in a convenient fixed location a means of bringing together, for social, spiritual, and intellectual stimulation, persons of varying nationality, race, and background, particularly students and others especially needing such contact.
2. To provide a neutral setting in which groups with conflicting interests, national or other, can meet for calm, informal discussion of common problems in a mutual attempt toward understanding.
3. To enable visitors from abroad to meet each other and to become acquainted with colleagues, officials, and others representatives of the host country.
4. To provide information and guidance needed by visitors from abroad, particularly students.

Characteristics include:

1. A specific building with meeting and recreational facilities, and a trained staff; usually subsidized by a sponsoring agency.
2. Living quarters included at some centers, especially at student international houses. Residence centers usually largely self-supporting.
3. Membership in international houses is usually divided into categories such as resident, nonresident, and alumni, with varying membership fees and privileges. Limit usually placed upon number of members of home nationality, usually between one-quarter and one-half of the total.
4. Larger student international houses linked informally and have transferable privileges and combined alumni association.
5. In case of Friends centers, religious motivation present but program nonsectarian and educational. Specific links maintained with Friends centers in other countries.
6. Usually closely related to the immediate community, a particular university, or a large international agency such as the United Nations.

7. Centers may be headquarters for relief or other social service and international projects in community, nation, or region.

Advantages claimed include:

1. Provides multinational, rather than mere binational, contacts.
2. Provides a ready basis for formation of lasting international friendships.
3. Self-government, as practiced in student international houses, provides lessons in democracy and training in international cooperation.
4. Permits national groups to make combined cultural contributions such as nationality dinners, national plays and dances, musical programs, etc.
5. May be valuable for short-term visitors, who otherwise lack opportunity for social and intellectual contacts.
6. Offers a ready source of information, guidance, and assistance to visitors needing such service.
7. Flexibility of objectives and program permits quick adaptation to meet special problems which community may present to certain groups of foreign visitors, such as those subject to race segregation.
8. May perform special service in bringing together officials and other persons for informal, off-the-record discussion of problems concerning which customary official or formal relationships are insufficient. Linked centers in different countries permit joint coordinated study of particular issues with provision for regular exchange of views and reporting of findings.

Factors sometimes overlooked:

1. Sometimes persons become isolated from local community, and visitors from abroad may obtain less contact with home life in host country through the temptation to associate either with an international group or with compatriots at the center.
2. May attract persons, particularly of host nationality, lacking good personality adjustment and using centers as escape from unsatisfying social relationships.

3. Residence centers tend to preoccupy staff with administrative details.
4. Extensive and varied program may distract from member's academic and other purposes, especially at the resident international houses.

Research and evaluation:

Each center has its own approach to evaluation, usually highly informal and stressing follow-up through correspondence of ex-members. The American Friends Service Committee is encouraging more comprehensive evaluation of its centers in the United States, Europe, and Asia.

A partial list of agencies with operating or coordinating experience:

AMERICAN COUNCIL ON EDUCATION, WASHINGTON INTERNATIONAL CENTER (mainly for orientation of foreign visitors and hospitality)
AMERICAN FRIENDS SERVICE COMMITTEE
INTERNATIONAL HOUSE ALUMNI ASSOCIATION
INTERNATIONAL HOUSES *in* New York, Chicago, Berkeley, Philadelphia, Washington, Boston (Cambridge), and elsewhere
International centers in many cities and universities

ORGANIZED EDUCATIONAL TRAVEL

Purposes include:

1. To permit acquisition, within relatively brief time, of wide range of cultural experience abroad, usually in several countries and stressing a particular problem or professional interest.
2. To provide the leavening influence of group experience to supplement individual impressions.
3. Occasionally, to obtain college or university credit.
4. To provide less expensive travel.

Characteristics include:

1. Tours arranged for groups by commercial and nonprofit agencies, the latter including professional organizations and educational institutions.

2. Concentration upon a field of interest, a professional objective, an international problem, a region, or a country.
3. Frequently involves participation in a special course, a conference, a seminar, a celebration, or other particular event.
4. Group consists of persons of similar interests and backgrounds; contacts provided with similar groups abroad.
5. Usually provides low-cost transportation and reduced rates throughout, occasionally in chartered plane or bus.
6. Guides generally experienced in countries visited and in special field of interest.
7. Often includes planned orientation and evaluation, usually on shipboard.

Advantages claimed include:

1. Provides relatively inexpensive, effortless travel, serving as an introduction to a region, problem, or international aspects of a professional field. Good background for later independent travel.
2. Combines sightseeing with educational and cultural experiences, sometimes carrying college credit.
3. Group appreciation and understanding of what is observed may be greater than that of individuals, with opportunity to correct erroneous individual impressions, particularly if orientation and evaluation programs are included.
4. Expert guidance enhances understanding and makes possible valuable contacts less readily available to individuals.
5. Results in close friendships of persons of common interests within the group, particularly if group is carefully selected.
6. Sponsorship by nonprofit professional group facilitates follow-up of professional experiences abroad and provides opportunity for developing supplementary cultural relations.

Factors sometimes overlooked:

1. Often difficult to distinguish in advance between professionally motivated nonprofit sponsors and those organized for commercial purposes. Some tours, particularly those organized for

profit, may be poorly directed and planned and not actually study tours as claimed.

2. Tendency to overstress exciting, rather than educational, experiences, and to touch countries and interests so superficially as to reinforce erroneous stereotypes.

3. More difficult than with other forms of interchange to create lasting friendships abroad because of time factor and demands of group.

4. Often difficult to provide adequate orientation of both travelers and hosts. Such orientation is needed to establish proper rapport between visitors and hosts, and to avoid disregard for mores of host country.

Research and evaluation:

Research and objective evaluation lacking, but need is generally recognized by the Council on Student Travel and other groups which hope to meet it, if funds become available. The Council for Correlation of International Educational Enterprises, now combined with the Council on Student Travel, sponsored, with the assistance of the Carnegie Endowment for International Peace, an unpublished study of travel experience, by Deming Hoyt. Many individual operating agencies are conducting continuous self-evaluations, and most tours include appraisal discussions at the end of the project and evaluative correspondence from participants.

A partial list of agencies with operating or coordinating experience:

The principal coordinating agency for student travel is the Council on Student Travel. This council issues a directory of student travel programs. Information about travel for teachers, other professional workers, farmers, trade union members, women's organizations, etc., is not currently coordinated, but may usually be obtained from the nonprofit travel agencies or from the leading professional organizations in each field. In addition, many universities, colleges, and schools sponsor educational travel.

Other agencies able to provide useful information include:

AFFILIATION OF SCHOOLS AND SEMINARS FOR INTERNATIONAL STUDY AND
    TRAVEL

AMERICAN TRAVEL ASSOCIATION

NATIONAL EDUCATION ASSOCIATION, DIVISION OF TRAVEL SERVICE

NATIONAL STUDENT ASSOCIATION

YOUTH ARGOSY, INC.

9.

Interchange of Materials

Most cultural relations projects sooner or later use, interchange, or provide books, equipment, and expendable supplies. Some projects also involve basic relief assistance, such as the provision of food, clothing, shelter, and medical supplies. Since the end of World War II, voluntary agencies have tended increasingly to treat interchange and provision of materials in international projects as supplementary to and by-products of other techniques and objectives. In 1946, when CIER launched its campaign for cultural assistance to devastated countries, it urged voluntary and governmental organizations to give high priority to services providing trained personnel, while continuing to encourage material assistance projects. The principal operating agencies providing material aid have gradually transferred their attention to cultural projects in which the provision of materials, if involved at all, is incidental to other objectives. However, interchange of materials will always remain an important element in cultural relations.

In view of the disparity among the three approaches described in this chapter, it is difficult to isolate common advantages and limitations. However, the following would seem to apply in most cases:

Advantages include:
1. Interchange of materials is a satisfying, tangible form of activity, relatively easy to administer and to follow up.
2. It is infinitely adaptable to all age levels and interests.
3. In case of supplies and equipment, such interchange eliminates language barriers.
4. Interchange of books and equipment constitutes a lasting reminder of good will.

5. Materials can provide basis for self-help.
6. Such interchange is a convenient and often necessary adjunct to other forms of cultural relations.
7. Problems of currency conversion of some countries may be partially overcome by gifts in kind.

Limitations include:

1. Needs and conditions change rapidly and shipment is often so slow that it is difficult to provide most essential items at the time needed.
2. Materials interchange is less likely than some other types of projects to admit of reciprocity, except for some publications exchanges, which may encounter language barriers. Projects stressing material aid run the risk of developing superior-inferior relationships or "charity" attitudes.
3. Relatively few agencies have field staff competent to check needs, oversee distribution, and follow up use.
4. Unless special provision is made for shared planning and careful reporting and follow-up, this approach may have fewer educational values to donors and recipients than personal services.
5. The cost of shipping may exceed the value of some items. Unless waived, tariff regulations increase costs.

Projects involving interchange of publications are clearly in a somewhat different category from those supplying other educational materials and equipment, or relief needs. Books and periodicals are an important reflection of a country's culture. They are produced in all countries, and, thus, mutual interchange of books is more readily possible than interchange of materials of other types.

Libraries, institutions, organizations, and individuals have for years exchanged their publications extensively, except when war has intervened. World War II interrupted the flow of publications seriously. As far as American publications abroad are concerned, the gap of the war years was partially filled through the effort of the American Book Center for War-Devastated Libraries (later converted into the U.S. Book Exchange). This private agency, located in the Library of Congress, was inaugurated in 1945 by the Council of National Library Associations, composed of the American Library Association and other leading library organizations. Since its inception, the U.S. Book Exchange has facilitated the sending of 250,000 books and periodicals, and remains the principal coordinating agency for work in this field. The Committee on International Scientific Publications of the National Research Council distributes abroad abstracts of scientific reports in technical journals. Within its field, the CARE Book Plan offers purchases at substantial reductions and supervision abroad by trained field staffs.

The major coordinating agency, or central clearinghouse of information for the sending of educational supplies and equipment, is the U.S. National Commission for UNESCO. UNESCO also maintains an office in New York providing similar services. Valuable information can be provided by the American Council of Voluntary Agencies for Foreign Service and by the Advisory Committee for Voluntary Foreign Aid, Department of State. In addition, several of the larger operating agencies have had considerable experience in transmitting educational materials and can provide helpful advice.

In some respects the most comprehensive material aid project is the UNESCO Gift Coupon Plan. A donor wishing to purchase a certain item for a purpose and a recipient specifically approved by UNESCO to receive such an item, accomplish the purpose by the donor buying and forwarding a special coupon which serves as a form of international currency. Actual purchase by the recipient is made through regular commercial channels. The plan stresses audio-visual equipment, scientific materials, publications, and vocational training equipment, but can also be used to provide scholarships.

Whether or not the provision of basic relief materials, such as food, clothing, and medical supplies, is considered a form of international cultural relations depends largely upon the emphasis upon cultural values in the planning and administration of projects. It is, however, possible to conduct even basic relief projects so as to produce lasting friendly relations with groups and individuals in recipient countries. This has been well demonstrated by the work of such agencies as the National Catholic Welfare Conference, the American Friends Service Committee, Church World Service, the Brethren Service Commission, and CARE. This possibility has been stressed in the gradual development of standards of good practice which relief agencies have been establishing under the guidance of the American Council of Voluntary Agencies and the Advisory Committee on Voluntary Foreign Aid of the Department of State.[1] It is significant that many projects which began with specific relief objectives have continued as cultural relations projects.

The addresses of the agencies mentioned above and in the subsections which follow are listed in the Appendix.

INTERCHANGE OF PUBLICATIONS

Purposes include:

1. To direct flow of books, pamphlets, periodicals, maps, and other printed materials to places needing them most.
2. To aid in reconstruction and development.
3. To provide better information about the country of origin—its culture and language.
4. To maintain interchange of latest research and thought in professional, technical, and cultural fields.

Characteristics vary widely with project, but often include:

1. Facilitation by sponsoring or coordinating agency of exchanges between libraries, institutions, or organized groups, of used and new printed materials.
2. Programs such as that of United States Book Exchange are

---

[1] Under the broadened scope of the Advisory Committee on Voluntary Foreign Aid, it was announced in 1952 that "Any person or nongovernmental organization or agency carrying on any nonprofit activities in the United States for the purpose of furthering or engaging in voluntary aid in areas outside the United States, including, but not limited to, projects and services of relief, rehabilitation, reconstruction and welfare in the fields of health, education, agriculture, and industry, emigration and resettlement, may voluntarily make application for registration. . . ."

often reciprocal, publications being both given and received, although not on a strictly one-for-one basis.

3. Especially in the case of assistance projects or those designated to meet a special need or problem, priority lists developed with advice of agency abroad, and information to donors both of what to send and what is not needed.
4. Increasingly includes close participation of agencies abroad in planning, administration, distribution, and follow-up.
5. Usually includes careful orientation of, and specific instructions to, donors.
6. Often employed as an important phase of planned follow-up of projects involving interchange of persons and groups, such as advisory missions and advanced study projects. Interchange of publications may also result in other forms of cultural co-operation, such as affiliations between institutions and organizations.
7. May involve abstracting service whereby research and other technical and professional materials are selected for translation and placement in journals at home and abroad, particularly in the natural sciences (Committee on International Scientific Publications).
8. May provide book-purchasing service, with substantial publishers' discounts, based upon priority lists developed abroad (CARE Book Plan, launched in collaboration with UNESCO).
9. May involve use of gift coupons (see UNESCO Gift Coupon Plan under "Provision of Educational Materials," page 146).
10. May include distribution of surplus, unsold copies, as well as used copies (Darien Book Aid Plan).

Advantages claimed include:

1. Opportunity for contact with most broadly representative aspects of another culture.
2. Permits international contact for persons unable to travel.
3. A simple and relatively inexpensive outlet for providing assistance to, and exchanging ideas with, individuals and groups abroad.

4. A relatively durable form of interchange, with benefits accruing over a period of years.
5. Convenient and impressive way to document technical progress in a country, and to share it with others needing such help.
6. Particularly adapted to growing interest in English language.
7. Pictorial and graphic materials and maps overcome language barrier.
8. Nonprofit purchase plans such as CARE usually involve substantial publishers' discounts and greatly reduce overhead.

Factors sometimes overlooked:

1. Emergency or short-term projects are sometimes developed too hastily, with inadequate definition of needs and administrative machinery, while long-term projects may interfere with established trade channels. Requests received from abroad usually based on out-of-date information concerning latest books.
2. Prices of books published in the United States are much higher than those of most other countries, although they tend to be most in demand.
3. Medium may tend to reach educated classes only.
4. Current literature may reflect distorted or biased view of a culture.
5. Language barrier limits interchange of most books and pamphlets to a relatively few countries with already existing language, historical, or cultural ties.

Research and evaluation:

The United States Book Exchange, CARE, the American Library Association, UNESCO, and the Committee on International Scientific Publications have attempted evaluations from time to time. The last-named committee reports studies of the use of its material abroad by correspondence and through statistical analysis of increased rate of requests.

The following articles by Alice Ball, of the United States Book Exchange, provide information in this field: "Costs of Serial Acquisition through United States Book Exchange," *Serial Slants,* April

1951; and "Library Additions at Small Cost," *American Association of University Professors Bulletin,* XXXVII (1951-52), 723-25.

In addition, the American Council of Voluntary Agencies for Foreign Service published, in June 1952, a report on the handling of books and periodicals by American agencies.

A partial list of agencies with operating or coordinating experience:

AMERICAN BOOK PUBLISHERS COUNCIL

AMERICAN COUNCIL OF VOLUNTARY AGENCIES FOR FOREIGN SERVICE (advisory)

AMERICAN JEWISH JOINT DISTRIBUTION COMMITTEE

AMERICAN LIBRARY ASSOCIATION

CARE BOOK PLAN (also provides educational, medical, and agricultural material in addition to children's and professional books)

CONGREGATIONAL CHRISTIAN SERVICE COMMISSION

DARIEN BOOK AID PLAN

LIBRARY OF CONGRESS

NATIONAL RESEARCH COUNCIL, COMMITTEE ON INTERNATIONAL SCIENTIFIC PUBLICATIONS

SMITHSONIAN INSTITUTION, INTERNATIONAL EXCHANGE SERVICE

UNITARIAN SERVICE COMMITTEE

UNITED STATES BOOK EXCHANGE

U.S. NATIONAL COMMISSION FOR UNESCO, COMMITTEE ON VOLUNTARY INTERNATIONAL ASSISTANCE

WORLD STUDENT SERVICE FUND

PROVISION OF EDUCATIONAL MATERIALS[2]

Purposes include:

1. To meet real educational needs in devastated or otherwise handicapped countries, and of institutions needing help in other countries by supplying educational, scientific, and cultural supplies and equipment.
2. To provide a concrete approach to developing and expressing humanitarian and international ideals.

---

[2] *See also* "Interchange of Publications," p. 142.

3. To use tangible gifts as basis for friendly cultural relations, and as means of extending educational opportunity to youth.

Characteristics include:

1. Needs and priorities determined with assistance of coordinating agency or operating organization with wide contacts abroad.
2. Generally demands utilization of an established operating agency to ensure adequate administration, field experience, and facilities for economical purchase, shipment, and delivery. Agency usually obtains tariff waiver.
3. Materials interchange often incidental to other forms of cultural relations, such as technical missions and affiliations.
4. May include provision of educational and cultural materials of all kinds, from simple school supplies to elaborate medical equipment and paintings. Books and lasting equipment tend now to be stressed rather than expendable items.
5. One major technique (UNESCO Gift Coupon Plan) enables donor groups to purchase and send coupons to recipient institutions in another country for purchase in that country of needed materials through regular trade channels, avoiding currency obstacles and necessity of shipping.
6. Another gift purchase plan stresses books, but is also applicable to certain types of other materials (CARE Book Plan).

Advantages claimed include:

1. Most tangible form of international action.
2. Adaptable to all age levels and interests.
3. Overcomes language barriers.
4. Provides "grease wherever the squeak is," if based upon careful study of actual needs.
5. May provide benefits for a period of years. Such gifts as duplicating machines and tools provide means of self-help.
6. Affords opportunity for many to share in planning and conduct of projects, including those in the receiving country.
7. Useful supplement to other forms of cultural relations.
8. CARE and UNESCO gift plans relieve donor of problems of purchasing, packing, and shipping.

Factors sometimes overlooked:

1. Difficulty, despite help of coordinating agencies, in ascertaining and keeping up-to-date constantly changing needs and priorities. Occasionally, gifts have tended to overstress expendables readily available abroad, items not suited to other educational methods, or items adapted only to use in mechanized societies. Trained field staff usually needed to appraise needs and their relation to available sources of assistance.
2. Inherently "donor-recipient" rather than "two-way" relationship, although supplementary projects may overcome this problem.
3. Expense and burden of shipping and packing, especially when competent agency is not utilized.
4. Difficulty of retaining identity of donor when distribution is centralized through large agency, although adequate reporting may overcome this problem.
5. Necessity of safeguards against diversion of gift into trade channels. Such diversion is rare, but can seriously damage relations when it occurs.

Research and evaluation:

The Commission for International Educational Reconstruction (CIER), in coordinating postwar efforts for voluntary international cultural and educational assistance to devastated countries, established general standards and simple techniques for self-evaluation which are still utilized by most operating agencies. It was not, however, in a position to conduct research studies. Its functions were taken over in 1949 by the U.S. National Commission for UNESCO, Committee on Educational Reconstruction, renamed in 1952 the Committee on Voluntary International Assistance. This and the UNESCO national commissions in other countries are constantly evaluating the UNESCO Gift Coupon Plan. The American Council of Voluntary Agencies for Foreign Service, the American Friends Service Committee, the National Education Association, and the American National Red Cross have attempted informal evaluations of projects of various types involving the sending of educational materials.

*A partial list of agencies with operating
or coordinating experience:*

AMERICAN COUNCIL OF VOLUNTARY AGENCIES FOR FOREIGN SERVICE
(advisory)
AMERICAN DENTAL ASSOCIATION
AMERICAN FEDERATION OF TEACHERS
AMERICAN FRIENDS SERVICE COMMITTEE
AMERICAN NATIONAL RED CROSS
ASSOCIATION FOR CHILDHOOD EDUCATION
BRETHREN SERVICE COMMISSION
CARE BOOK PLAN (books principally, but also medical, agricultural,
and educational materials)
CAMP FIRE GIRLS
DEPARTMENT OF STATE, ADVISORY COMMITTEE ON VOLUNTARY FOREIGN
AID (advisory)
NATIONAL CATHOLIC WELFARE CONFERENCE
NATIONAL CONGRESS OF PARENTS AND TEACHERS
NATIONAL COUNCIL OF THE CHURCHES OF CHRIST IN THE U.S.A., CENTRAL
DEPARTMENT OF CHURCH WORLD SERVICE
NATIONAL EDUCATION ASSOCIATION OF THE UNITED STATES
UNITED STATES BOOK EXCHANGE
U.S. NATIONAL COMMISSION FOR UNESCO (advisory)
WALDORF SCHOOLS FUND, INC.

BASIC RELIEF AS AN APPROACH TO CULTURAL RELATIONS

Purposes include:

1. To provide food, clothing, medicines, and other needed items
   to individuals and groups in distressed areas most needing them.
2. To provide goods essential to making services effective.
3. To conduct the distribution of basic relief so as to build hope
   and confidence in the future, and to lay basis for moral rehabilitation and lasting good will.

Characteristics include:

1. Sponsorship by private agencies, many of them religious.
2. Financial support by a large number of individual donors.
3. Trained professional social or health workers, supplemented by
   volunteers.

4. Aid usually given on basis of individual need, without reference to religious or other connection.
5. Usually administered in close collaboration with governments and local authorities.
6. Long-term cultural relations increasingly sought as important by-product through introduction of educational assistance, community activities, interchange of persons, affiliations, technical missions, etc.
7. Coordination achieved through consultation with American Council of Voluntary Agencies for Foreign Service and the Advisory Committee on Voluntary Foreign Aid of the Department of State.

Advantages claimed include:

1. Need for food, clothing, shelter, and health must be met before other human values can be achieved.
2. Provides a simple, elemental basis of communication and understanding, satisfying both to donor and to recipient.
3. Voluntary relief projects are more likely to add the human touch and to promote cultural relations as a by-product than are large governmental or intergovernmental programs.
4. Relief-type projects, particularly those under voluntary auspices, demonstrate humanitarianism and are less likely to be suspected of ulterior or political motives.
5. When conducted in close cooperation with indigenous agencies and when careful follow-up is included in the plan, can be an excellent point of departure for other cultural relations activities.

Factors sometimes overlooked:

1. Need may exceed capacity and resources of agency, since the approach usually involves expendable goods needed in large quantities and over a long period of time.
2. When government and intergovernmental projects are involved, it is sometimes difficult to establish a clear role for private effort.
3. Unearmarked giving is more equitable than specifying recipients in advance, but it is difficult to keep donor informed and interested.

4. "Man cannot live by bread alone."
5. Inherently a unilateral approach, unless supplemented by cultural projects.

Research and evaluation:

While in essence a humanitarian activity and an act of faith, increasingly, objective standards have been developed for relief projects by the American Council of Voluntary Agencies for Foreign Service, the Advisory Committee on Voluntary Foreign Aid of the Department of State, and the several leading operating agencies. These standards tend to be consistent with established social welfare practices. The use of relief projects as a means to cultural relations has been the subject of numerous subjective case studies.

A partial list of agencies with operating or coordinating experience:

AMERICAN COUNCIL OF VOLUNTARY AGENCIES FOR FOREIGN SERVICE (advisory)

AMERICAN FRIENDS SERVICE COMMITTEE

BRETHREN SERVICE COMMISSION

CARE

DEPARTMENT OF STATE, ADVISORY COMMITTEE ON VOLUNTARY FOREIGN AID (advisory)

GENERAL FEDERATION OF WOMEN'S CLUBS

GREEK WAR RELIEF ASSOCIATION, INC., U.S.A., and the various denominational service committees and agencies working on behalf of particular countries or groups

AMERICAN JUNIOR RED CROSS

NATIONAL CATHOLIC EDUCATIONAL ASSOCIATION

NATIONAL COUNCIL OF THE CHURCHES OF CHRIST IN THE U.S.A., CENTRAL DEPARTMENT OF CHURCH WORLD SERVICE

NATIONAL COUNCIL OF JEWISH WOMEN

SAVE THE CHILDREN FEDERATION, INC.

10.

Affiliations

THE "AFFILIATIONS URGE," as it has sometimes been termed, is a very general and understandable phenomenon in international cultural relations. It has at times taken the form of an emphasis upon "adoption" of individuals, institutions, and communities, as a humanitarian response to the material and spiritual needs of persons in need. Immediately following World War II, schools and colleges, in particular, were inclined to respond to appeals by offering to adopt particular institutions abroad.

The concept of "adoption" was soon found to be too limited, implying attitudes of condescension, too likely to create undue expectation of large-scale assistance. It has been virtually abandoned in favor of the more flexible concept of "affiliation," which implies a linking between groups with similar interests for mutual advantage.

Such linking of educational institutions for mutual advantage has been going on for many years. Missionary efforts resulting in the establishment of educational institutions have long employed the technique of asking denominational American colleges and churches to "adopt" institutions in the mission fields. Independently of religious motivation, other higher institutions have at times taken the lead in strengthening educational opportunities abroad. Yale-in-China and colleges started and financed by American agencies in the Near East have for several generations provided important training of future leaders in their areas.

Similarly, civic, professional, fraternal, and labor groups and other types of organizations with common purposes have tended to affiliate, often formally through joint membership in inter-

151

national organizations. Affiliation with "internationals" has become a commonplace of the American organization pattern.

Affiliation of schools, higher institutions, organizations, and communities has several advantages as compared with other forms of cultural relations.

Advantages commonly ascribed to affiliations:

1. Combines group-to-group with person-to-person relationships.
2. Utilizes natural, normal, continuing units—institutions, organizations, communities.
3. Facilitates programs requiring sustained effort.
4. Provides a convenient springboard for all forms of cultural relations.
5. Involves an inherently mutual relationship, with both parties benefiting in tangible ways.

Limitations commonly ascribed to affiliations:

1. Homogeneity, congeniality, and common background difficult to arrange.
2. Great tact and skill in administration required.
3. Completely mutual understanding of purposes and desired outcomes is rare. Material aid too often anticipated.
4. Termination of unsatisfactory affiliations often involves keen disappointment to one party or both, and may cause ill will.

In contrast to the group projects discussed in the preceding chapter, there are few agencies capable of offering comprehensive information about affiliations. However, at least one agency for each of the major types of affiliation offers a medium of coordinating service, with the exception of affiliation of organizations. The School Affiliations Service of the American Friends Service Committee is one of the principal sources of information and guidance in its field. For university affiliations, the World Student Service Fund (affiliate of the World University Service) performs a similar, although more limited, function. For community affiliations, Operation Democracy is a major source of information.

However, each of these agencies serves only a relatively small number of countries in its affiliations work.

Such coordinating agencies as the U.S. National Commission for UNESCO and the American Council of Voluntary Agencies for Foreign Service provide additional sources of information. The Institute of International Education, the American Council on Education, and the National Education Association have also had experience with affiliations, or at least with closely related projects. The Department of State and the U.S. Office of Education are additional sources of information.

The above agencies and those listed in the subsections which follow are listed with their addresses in the Appendix.

AFFILIATIONS BETWEEN ORGANIZATIONS

Purposes include:

1. To unite with groups of similar interest and background for achievement of common international perspectives and goals.
2. To provide a regular channel for interchange of experiences.
3. To facilitate interchanges of persons and materials.
4. To develop within the organizations a sense of world-wide community of interests.
5. To establish international relationships on a basis of mutuality and of reasonable equivalence.

Characteristics include:

1. Long-term links between groups with common interests, either through joint membership in international bodies or through bilateral fraternal relationship.
2. Usually includes correspondence, exchange of publications, collaboration in joint projects, joint participation in conferences, and fraternal contacts through intervisitation.
3. Includes assistance projects, when needed, on behalf of needy affiliated groups and individuals.
4. Applies in some form to organizations of all types, including youth, civic, religious, professional, labor, farm, fraternal, and business.

5. Often involves regular annual or biennial international conferences or congresses in the case of many international agencies with national affiliates.
6. International nongovernmental organizations used increasingly as advisers by the U.N. and its specialized agencies.

Advantages claimed include:
1. Inherent mutuality, equivalence, and spontaneity.
2. Relatively little administrative machinery and expense.
3. Avoidance of self-conscious striving for "good will" as end in itself, since it involves joining together for a common goal.
4. Convenient means for interchange of professional and technical information and research.
5. Convenient starting point for other forms of international cultural relations, and for their follow-up.

Factors sometimes overlooked:
1. Disparity between countries in professional standards, interests, and resources, handicapping participation on equal basis.
2. Language barriers, causing overstress upon relations between groups in a few countries of common background.
3. Danger of domination, or suspected domination, by particularly strong affiliates in certain countries, particularly those in United States.
4. Danger of overstress upon sentimental values and publicity.

Research and evaluation:
No objective, external research or evaluation have been reported, but many agencies have elaborate programs for review and self-evaluation, often through international relations committees.

Operating agencies and sources of information:
No general operating agencies or central clearinghouse of information concerning organization affiliations. Dates of important international professional meetings are listed in UNESCO's *Official Bulletin* and in the *Bulletin* of the Union of International Associations, Brussels.

SCHOOL AFFILIATIONS

Purposes include:

1. To develop link for mutual stimulation and educational enrichment between schools of similar type and interest in different countries.
2. To serve as foundation for cultural relations projects of other types.

Characteristics include:

1. Involves careful period of preparation, using qualified professional staff at home and abroad, when affiliations are arranged by national sponsoring agencies.
2. "Ground rules" usually emphasize mutuality, avoidance of donor-recipient relationship, all-school involvement, conditions of continuation and termination, etc., agreed to by both schools.
3. Contact initiated through group or personal correspondence, followed by exchange of classroom work.
4. May eventually result in other forms of interchange often including intervisitation, exchange of students and teachers, joint work camps, teachers conferences, etc.
5. Affiliations supervised by professional field workers, who watch for potentialities for expansion or signs of flagging interest, and propose changes or new stimuli if difficulties seem to be arising.
6. Closely related to curriculum and extracurricular activities.
7. Costs to individual schools usually modest, especially if sponsoring agency receives outside subsidy.

Advantages claimed include:

1. Valuable adjunct to school program, particularly social studies and languages.
2. Inherently reciprocal relationship.
3. International experience for youth on common interest level, involving groups relatively homogeneous in age and academic development.
4. Intensive contact with one school and country, providing valuable insights into habits, customs, and basic values.

5. Tangible approach, making it a good steppingstone for projects of other types and involving other countries.
6. Convenient technique for promoting community-school co-operation in an international project.

Factors sometimes overlooked:

1. Unless way is carefully prepared by professional staff, schools may not be properly matched. Basis of affiliation may otherwise be misunderstood.
2. Relatively expensive central administration by sponsoring agency is required.
3. Continuity of local administration and correspondence are sometimes hard to provide.
4. Enthusiasm may wane more rapidly in one of affiliated schools, especially if the project depends largely upon efforts of a single leader. Such changes in attitude may result in disappointment and embitterment.
5. Unless supplemented by other approaches, affiliation may tend to narrow students' interest to a single school, community, or country abroad.

Research and evaluation:

The School Affiliation Service of the American Friends Service Committee is undertaking to evaluate its experience since 1946, utilizing as consultants leading educators and psychologists. Questions it is endeavoring to answer include: Are some by-products of affiliations more important in changing attitudes than basic program? Which projects have most impact on individual participants and school community? Is impact greater with elementary or secondary pupils? Is greater emphasis upon contact with teachers or pupils justified? In what sense is the School Affiliation Service a "pilot" project? What part of our experience could be shared with other schools? In what form? To what ends? Is the trend toward greater or less dependence of affiliated schools on personal staff aid, and is the trend salutary?

*A partial list of agencies with operating
or coordinating experience:*

AMERICAN FRIENDS SERVICE COMMITTEE, SCHOOL AFFILIATION SERVICE
SAVE THE CHILDREN FEDERATION, INC.

UNIVERSITY AND COLLEGE AFFILIATIONS
*Linking of Particular Institutions, or Divisions
Thereof, in Different Countries*

Purposes include:

1. To create on the part of students, faculty, and administration, an effective sense of international responsibility by focusing attention upon a single institution or a small number of affiliated institutions.
2. To provide mutual stimulation and enrichment of educational programs.
3. To permit intensive study of, and relations with, a single institution so that more tangible progress may be achieved than when interests are scattered widely.
4. To provide a desirable springboard for later broadening of concern for institutions in other regions.

Characteristics include:

1. Stresses mutuality and long-term relationships.
2. May involve either an all-institution affiliation, or may be limited to student bodies, faculty, or particular schools or departments.
3. Stresses material assistance more frequently than is usual with school affiliations.
4. Often includes exchange of professors and students.
5. Almost always includes exchange of publications.
6. Sometimes necessitates special grants of funds from foundations, organizations, or individuals.
7. Particularly common between specialized institutions, especially teachers colleges.
8. May be arranged through a national service agency (usually

the World Student Service Fund), a religious organization, or
on the initiative of administration, faculty, or students.

Advantages claimed include:

1. Mobilizes responsible concern for international affairs of a
   wider group of students and faculty than can participate in
   other forms of interchange.
2. Is an inherently reciprocal approach.
3. Supplements curriculum, particularly modern language, international relations, history, and comparative education, but also
   other social sciences, humanities, and natural sciences.
4. Renders other cultural relations and assistance projects more
   tangible and meaningful by focusing attention upon a particular institution abroad, and stimulates interest in such extracurricular activities as international relations clubs, campaigns
   of relief agencies, language clubs, international seminars, and
   work camps.
5. May open up special opportunities for planned interchange of
   faculty and students, and for better utilization on campus of
   visiting professors and students.
6. Develops better understanding of all aspects of life in a foreign
   country through intensive contact with particular institutions—
   supplementing usual study of political, historical, and economic
   factors—by direct contact with psychological, social, and ideological elements.
7. Provides a "home base" abroad for traveling students and
   faculty.
8. Provides a convenient means of involving alumni and community in purposeful, humanitarian international endeavor.
9. When carefully planned, may be a means of providing technical
   aid to institutions in underdeveloped areas over a period of
   years.

Factors sometimes overlooked:

1. Need for adequate coordinating service with trained field staff
   in order to base affiliations upon careful study of mutual in-

terests and needs and to ensure full understanding by both parties of affiliation. This need is largely met in the case of affiliated denominational colleges, and by World Student Service Fund in linking German and American universities. Adequate coordinating service is expensive.

2. Difficulty in selecting a single affiliate, when varied international contacts and interests are present. On the other hand, several affiliations or different affiliations in different departments may involve excessive diffusion of efforts and superficiality of contact.
3. Need for clearly defined, fully authorized, responsible, continuing group in each institution to provide sound planning and administration.
4. Need for early supplementation by "face-to-face" contact if affiliation is to take root.
5. Difficulty in terminating unsatisfactory affiliations without creating dissatisfaction by one party.

Research and evaluation:

Informal evaluation by World Student Service Fund and by committees of faculties and student bodies or both in several affiliated institutions, for example, Stanford University, University of Chicago, Michigan State College, and Columbia University.

A partial list of agencies with operating or coordinating experience:

AMERICAN ASSOCIATION OF COLLEGES FOR TEACHER EDUCATION
AMERICAN COUNCIL ON EDUCATION
CHURCH WORLD SERVICE
INSTITUTE OF INTERNATIONAL EDUCATION
NATIONAL CATHOLIC EDUCATIONAL ASSOCIATION
WORLD STUDENT SERVICE FUND (United States affiliate of World University Service)
Numerous individual institutions, including Yale University, Columbia University, University of Chicago, and Michigan State College

COMMUNITY AFFILIATIONS

Purposes include:

1. To link two comparable communities in different countries for purposes of cultural cooperation, and mutual education and stimulation.
2. To bring into direct relationship all major segments of each community—youth, professional workers, civic leaders, labor, churches, etc.
3. To provide basis for all forms of cultural relations, and possibly also for material assistance, if needed.

Characteristics include:

1. Affiliations usually initiated by action of local organizations, sometimes by exchange of letters between mayors, often with help of a national agency.
2. Principal organizations in both cities, such as town councils, civic groups, and chambers of commerce involved.
3. Affiliations began with relief objective, but now stress long-term cultural relations.
4. Early affiliations tended to stress similarity of name, or links between places of origin of early settlers in United States, i.e., Dunkirk to Dunkerque, New Rochelle and La Rochelle, but other basis found for most recent affiliations.
5. Communities are usually comparable in populations and cultural interests.
6. Affiliations most common between American communities and those in France, Germany, and other European countries, although potentially available in any accessible country.
7. Plan often includes correspondence between schools and organizations, exchange of gifts, relief assistance when needed, public ceremonies, art exhibits, fairs, musical events, and interchange of "good-will ambassadors."
8. Sometimes involves counties, particularly in Kansas, where county UNESCO commissions have taken the initiative.

Advantages claimed include:

1. Provides basis for comprehensive understanding of local culture and problems through intensive, all-community approach.
2. Permits better visualization of outcomes of cultural relations projects than with more general approach.
3. Involves large number of local agencies and individuals, including both those not ordinarily concerned with international affairs and those already having international contacts.
4. Enriches educational programs of schools and organizations.
5. Widens international horizons of local groups, resulting in interest in other places and regions and approaches.

Factors sometimes overlooked:

1. May be unduly influenced by enthusiasm of a few energetic individuals without adequate local backing or ability to follow through.
2. Selection of affiliate may stress importance of historical or sentimental factors rather than commonality of interest.
3. Tends to stress ties with a few countries, largely those with close existing cultural links, although affiliations with the Middle East, Far East, and South America are now being established.
4. For groups having existing international ties and commitments, may involve, at least temporarily, a narrowing of interests.
5. When no international body assists in making primary contacts to assure correct interpretation, difficult to establish on a basis of complete mutuality and full understanding of implications. Difficult to avoid possible misunderstanding of motives or undue expectation of material aid. Economic differences may make reciprocity difficult, unless only "token gifts" are specified.
6. Difficult to terminate or revive during a "lull" without incurring ill will on the part of the more active party.

Research and evaluation:

Operation Democracy, Inc., follows up affiliations with reports and evaluations, keeping records on each town from year to year, with periodic reports to the State Department. Bulletins are issued listing and describing affiliations. Steering committees in each community are encouraged to appraise results and trends periodically.

Operating agencies and sources of information include:

Several operating agencies have employed this approach from time to time and one active national organization is devoted wholly to it—Operation Democracy, Inc., which terms its program "cultural affiliations with token gifts." Its services are offered without charge to communities developing affiliations. The Medway Plan also provides "town adoptions" along with other international projects. Among the communities that have developed affiliations, or which have established affiliations committees, since the war (some more active than others) are:

Albany, N.Y.—Nijmegen, Holland; Atchison County, Kan.—Bhavnagar, India; Aurora, Ohio—El Marj, Lebanon; Barber County, Kan.—Clervaux, Luxembourg; Barton County, Kan.—Phlorina, Greece; Baton Rouge, La.—Cairo, Egypt; Bloomfield, Neb.—Kamen, Germany; Bronxville, N.Y.—Sarreguemines, France; Brooklyn, N.Y.—Breukelen, Holland; Butler County, Kan.—Beaugency, France; Cedar Grove, N.J.—Vilshofen, Germany; Chester, N.J.—Kumrovac, Yugoslavia; Cincinnati, Ohio—Munich, Germany; Dunkirk, N.Y.—Dunkerque, France, and Anzio, Italy; Edwards County, Kan.—Dieuze, Vergaville, Blanche-Eglise, and Gueblange-les-Dieuze, France; Faribault, Minn.—Würzburg, Germany; Ford County, Kan.—Nykobing-Falster, Denmark; Garden City, N.Y.—Coburg, Germany and Aix-en-Provence, France; Glen Cove, N.Y.—Pontecorvo, Italy; Greensburg, Ky.—Staltach, Germany; Hilo, Hawaii—Hiroshima, Japan; Hudson, Ohio—Soubrug, Holland; Hyde Park, N.Y.—Lannoy, France; Independence, Mo.—Annecy, France; Jersey City, N.J.—Capracotta, Italy; Kalamazoo, Mich.—Fougères, France; Kokomo, Ind.—Amberg, Germany; Larchmont, N.Y.—Abbeville, France; Mamaroneck, N.Y.—Amersfoort, Holland; Maplewood, N.J.—Vianden, Luxembourg; Meadville, Pa.—Fismes, France; Mentor, Ohio—Suolahti, Finland; Millburn, N.J.—Bergues, France; Montclair, N.J.—Graz, Austria; Monroe, La.—Ingolstadt, Germany; Morganville, Kan.—Feves, France; Neosho County, Kan.—Zevenbergen, Holland; Pittsburg, Kan.—Bergen, Norway; Rhinebeck, N.Y.—Waldorf, Germany; Ridgewood, N.J.—Nurri, Italy; Rye, N.Y.—Rye, England; San Francisco, Calif.—Caen, France; Scarsdale, N.Y.—Wissembourg, France; Seattle, Wash.—San Gimignano, Italy; St. Cloud, Minn.—Mellrichstadt, Germany; Storrs Branch, Conn.—Weyer, Upper Austria; Tucson, Ariz.—Tucson and Trikkala, Greece; Wellesley, Mass.—Vilshofen, Germany; Westbury, N.Y.—Corregio, Italy; Weston, Mass.—Rombas, France; Westport, Conn.—Marigny, France; Wichita, Kan.—Orléans, France; Worcester, Mass.—Worcester, England; Worthington, Minn.—Crailsheim, Germany.

11.

Other Approaches

THE APPROACHES AND the techniques dealt with in this chapter (correspondence, American-supported institutions abroad, interchange in the fine arts, and orientation and hospitality centers) are not readily classifiable under any of the broad headings of affiliations or interchanges of individuals, groups, or materials. They all relate, however, in a measure to one or more of these large classifications.

Correspondence is, of course, a form of interchange between individuals, although it does not involve actual movement of persons. American-supported schools abroad are, in a sense, group projects and affiliations, not necessarily, however, involving movement of organized groups to other countries, or formal affiliations between institutions. Interchange in the arts may employ almost every other approach, but the stress is on techniques unique to the arts.

Orientation courses and hospitality programs are techniques employed in interchange of persons and groups. They are actually special services supplementing such interchange, often sponsored by agencies other than those administering the projects described in chapters 7 and 8. Orientation and hospitality might be treated under some such heading as "Community Approaches to International Cultural Relations," but since this classification would suggest many activities not involving actual contact with persons or groups from abroad, it did not seem a suitable way in which to organize the present discussion. This classification would necessitate inclusion of all sorts of community, school, college, and adult programs relating to international affairs, such as exhibits, concerts, fairs, dramatic performances, conferences on world problems, and foreign student advisement. Worth-while and significant as these are, they require separate treatment.

A good case could be made for including in this chapter other special techniques which were included somewhat arbitrarily under the headings of preceding chapters. For example, the "Experiment in International Living" included under chapter 7 is a technique with special characteristics, not found in other projects. The same may be said for the Lisle Fellowship under chapter 8, the New York Herald Tribune High School Forum under chapter 7, and the American Junior Red Cross, included under chapter 9, and for several others. Any grouping tends to do violence to unique and valuable special approaches such as these. To deal fully with the program of any one of the many agencies doing unusual or pioneer work in a field as broad as international cultural relations was beyond the scope of this study.

In this chapter devoted to "unclassifiable" approaches and techniques, it is obviously impossible to attempt a listing of common advantages and limitations.

The addresses of the agencies mentioned above and in the subsections which follow are to be found in the Appendix.

CORRESPONDENCE PROJECTS

Purposes include:
1. To promote international friendship on a "person-to-person" basis.
2. To provide means for those unable to travel to make direct contacts abroad.
3. To exchange information, experience, and ideas with persons of different nationality, and to replace wrong stereotypes with more accurate impressions.
4. To enrich understanding of school subjects.

Characteristics include:
1. Links established between persons of different nationality but of similar age, background, and interests. Often organized by a sponsoring agency, school, or teacher.

2. Costs low, even if sponsoring agency charges fee.
3. Correspondence also carried on between groups.
4. Little supervision provided, or feasible, after contact is established, except sometimes within school.
5. Supplements school program, particularly study of English, French, German, Spanish, and social studies.
6. Tendency to be limited to relations between persons in countries having close linguistic, political, and cultural ties.

Advantages claimed include:

1. Way of providing international cultural relations for large numbers of young persons and persons unable to travel.
2. Simple and inexpensive.
3. Intimate personal contact may result more readily than from ordinary travel. Lifelong friendships may be formed.
4. Means of stimulating interest in school subjects, particularly languages and social studies.
5. Infinite adaptability to varying interests, age groups, background, and nationalities.
6. Subtle way of dispelling false impressions of a people and strengthening political as well as cultural links.

Factors sometimes overlooked:

1. Extremely difficult to supervise. Oversentimentalism, ulterior motives such as desire for individual personal assistance, may be hard to control. Even when relief assistance is justified, objective check on need is usually impossible.
2. Difficult to keep on a basis of complete mutuality. When one party loses interest, the other may be embittered. Needs to be continually motivated.
3. Correspondence between groups difficult to organize and maintain.
4. Language barrier limits contact, excluding many countries.
5. Need for careful planning and orientation, dependable sponsorship in both countries, and complete understanding by both parties of objectives, pitfalls, and "ground rules"—all difficult to provide.

Research and evaluation:

Much more study of this technique is needed. Reports indicate general lack of careful evaluation and of adequately financed, professional coordinating services. The U.S. Office of Education has operated an extensive project, and now issues an annotated list of agencies. The National Education Association's Committee on International Relations is planning to set up a series of pilot projects to examine the results of international correspondence.

A partial list of agencies with operating or coordinating experience:

ENGLISH-SPEAKING UNION, PEN FRIENDS DIVISION

FÉDÉRATION INTERNATIONALE DES ORGANISATIONS DE CORRESPONDANCE ET D'ECHANGES SCOLAIRES (FIOCES; an international association operating through member bureaus)

INTERNATIONAL FRIENDSHIP LEAGUE

INTERNATIONAL STUDENTS SOCIETY

NATIONAL BUREAU OF EDUCATIONAL CORRESPONDENCE

NATIONAL EDUCATION ASSOCIATION OF THE UNITED STATES, COMMITTEE ON INTERNATIONAL RELATIONS, UNITED NATIONS EDUCATION SERVICE

STUDENT FORUM ON INTERNATIONAL RELATIONS

STUDENT LETTER EXCHANGE (member of Fédération Internationale des Organisations de Correspondance et d'Echanges Scolaires)

U.S. OFFICE OF EDUCATION

YOUTH OF ALL NATIONS, INC.

AMERICAN-SUPPORTED INSTITUTIONS ABROAD

Purposes include:

1. To provide needed educational opportunities to people of a country or region, or
2. To provide education under religious auspices, or
3. To maintain institutions as "outposts" of American language and culture, for use by Americans in residence or by natives desiring an American education, or a combination of these three.

Characteristics vary widely with purpose, location, and educational level, but each of the following applies to at least some institutions:

1. All depend largely, although rarely entirely, upon private financial aid from United States, usually provided by an American sponsoring institution or agency. In Latin America, American schools also receive modest United States government assistance, and in countries covered by the Fulbright Act, they may receive indirect assistance through grants to American teachers.
2. Includes elementary schools, secondary schools, colleges, universities, vocational schools, and special schools.
3. Particularly numerous in Latin America, Near East, and missionary fields of Asia and Africa.
4. Generally aspires to gradually increasing local and national participation in financing and control.
5. Increasingly include institutions in so-called underdeveloped areas for technical assistance.
6. Usually includes nationals of country in staffs and student bodies.

Advantages claimed include:

1. Highly personalized contacts with an area provided to donors through provision for full and regular reporting.
2. American-type schools with instruction in English bring students abroad into contact with American education, provide opportunity for others to learn our language, and creates basis for long-term cultural ties.
3. May serve needs of American children abroad, particularly those intending to complete their education in the United States.
4. Outlet for persons well qualified for teaching abroad, but unable for language or other reasons to serve in native schools.
5. Private agencies often better able to enlist local cooperation than are official government projects.
6. Denominational organizations can often best maintain both religious and social services programs by maintaining their own educational institutions abroad.

7. May be a convenient means of providing technical aid, since American teachers usually remain for relatively long periods and can sometimes function best in the familiar atmosphere of an American-sponsored institution.

Factors sometimes overlooked:

1. Institutions established on American educational pattern may take insufficient cognizance of local conditions and needs. This factor may be partially overcome by joint planning with domestic agencies.
2. May depend too long upon outside help, instead of seeking ways of increasing local self-help.
3. Expensive services and financing by voluntary contributions in the United States may be undependable. Institutions sometimes launched before adequate funds are assured and programs curtailed suddenly may damage good will.
4. Largely a one-way relationship, serving a group abroad, although values to donors and sponsors may also accrue.

Research and evaluation:

Each agency has its own criteria and approach to evaluation, usually highly subjective. The Near East Foundation, the American Council on Education, and the several denominational agencies are continuously appraising their programs. The Department of State is endeavoring to evaluate such projects along with others.

A partial list of agencies with operating or coordinating experience:

AMERICAN COUNCIL ON EDUCATION, INTER-AMERICAN SCHOOLS SERVICE
BRITISH-AMERICAN FOUNDATION FOR EUROPEAN EDUCATION
DEPARTMENT OF STATE, INTERNATIONAL INFORMATION ADMINISTRATION
JAPANESE INTERNATIONAL CHRISTIAN UNIVERSITY FOUNDATION
NEAR EAST COLLEGE ASSOCIATION
NEAR EAST FOUNDATION
U.S. DEPARTMENT OF THE ARMY (for schools for United States dependents, especially in Germany, Japan, and Austria)
WALDORF SCHOOLS FUND, INC.

The various religious bodies, particularly those sponsoring missionary schools

INTERCHANGE IN THE FINE ARTS

Purposes vary widely with type of project and nature of sponsorship, but usually include:

1. To employ this universal and inherently international form of expression to build and strengthen international relations.
2. To provide better appreciation of the cultural aspects of life in each country.
3. Indirectly, to combat erroneous stereotypes of a people, particularly the view held abroad that the United States has no contribution to make to the arts.

Characteristics vary widely with the project, art form, and auspices, but may include:

1. Sponsorship by national, international, or local agencies and organizations.
2. Art forms ranging from graphic arts, music, drama, the dance, to architecture, and all forms of aesthetic expression and appreciation having significance to more than one country.
3. Methods ranging from exchange of classroom paintings to vast international theater and music festivals, and may include exhibits, lectures, exchanges of artists, competitions, and aid to needy artists abroad.
4. Wide cost range for different types of projects. Export of dramatic and musical productions expensive.

Advantages claimed include:

1. Art interchange most inherently international form of cultural relations. "Art knows no boundaries."
2. Mutual participation in, or appreciation of, arts among the easiest ways of reducing tensions between hostile groups and promoting reconciliation between persons of historically antagonistic nationality.
3. More completely than any other form of cultural relations, overcomes language barriers (with exception of drama).
4. All countries can participate on a basis of reasonably equivalent

mutual contribution, with the United States often having more to gain than to give. Excellent balance wheel for technical assistance and other cultural relations approaches which are necessarily less reciprocal.
5. A whole people can be involved in this approach, regardless of age, economic, or social level, or education, since all can appreciate and most take active part in some form of artistic experience.
6. A particularly effective way of developing international contacts between children, thus creating world-mindedness, and revealing their basic aspirations, fears, and acculturation.

Factors sometimes overlooked:

1. Excessive cost of some forms of art interchange, particularly dramatic and musical productions. Most forms cannot hope to be self-supporting.
2. Differing artistic tastes and standards in different countries, particularly in relation to new forms of expression.
3. Boastfulness or patronizing attitude in presentation of American art abroad would be particularly resented and self-defeating.
4. Needed government assistance lacking in the United States.
5. Lack of proper emphasis on the contribution the United States can make in field of arts in general education.

Research and evaluation:

Less susceptible than other forms of international relations to evaluation. However, response to such presentations as the German and Austrian art exhibits in the United States and United States musical dramatic productions abroad have been appraised statistically. The box office may be a poor test for some forms of artistic presentation.

A partial list of agencies with operating or coordinating experience:

AMERICAN ASSOCIATION OF MUSEUMS
AMERICAN FEDERATION OF ARTS

AMERICAN NATIONAL RED CROSS (for art correspondence and music interchange by children and youth)

AMERICAN NATIONAL THEATER AND ACADEMY

AMERICAN SYMPHONY ORCHESTRA LEAGUE, INC.

GUGGENHEIM FOUNDATION

INSTITUTE OF INTERNATIONAL EDUCATION (for interchange of persons)

NATIONAL ARTS FOUNDATION

NATIONAL EDUCATION ASSOCIATION OF THE UNITED STATES

   MUSIC EDUCATORS NATIONAL CONFERENCE

   NATIONAL ART EDUCATION ASSOCIATION

U.S. NATIONAL COMMISSION FOR UNESCO (advisory)

WOMEN'S INTERNATIONAL LEAGUE FOR PEACE AND FREEDOM (for school art interchange)

ORIENTATION COURSES

Purposes include:

1. To provide visitors from other countries with general information about, and an understanding of, the social and cultural institutions of the country visited, serving as a background for and supplement to their specialized studies and to facilitate their adjustment.
2. To enable visitors to test and strengthen the adequacy of their command of the language.
3. To provide an informal, friendly introduction to the people and customs of the host country.

Characteristics include:

1. Courses may range in length from a day or two to an entire year, most commonly taking the form either of (*a*) special six-week summer courses for students, (*b*) one-week courses for older visitors coming for only a few months, (*c*) a day or two of "briefing," (*d*) year-long courses in universities for general and language orientation, (*e*) shipboard programs.
2. Courses generally informal and optional, but sometimes a part of regular curriclum or projects.
3. Generally operated by nonofficial agencies—colleges, univer-

sities, or voluntary organizations, sometimes with the help of government funds, sometimes at own expense.

4. Courses stress customs and basic factors in the history, culture, and institutions of host country. Longer summer programs for students sponsored by the Institute of International Education jointly with cooperating higher institutions, include language refresher program. Usually include field trips, joint recreation, and hospitality.

5. Increasingly, where leadership is available, brief programs prior to the visitor's departure from his own country are conducted, and some orientation may be attempted by correspondence.

6. Special programs on student ships, particularly prevalent immediately following the war, oriented both United States students on early eastbound passage and European students on early westbound passage, with similar evaluation programs on return trips.

7. Orientation programs for older visitors established soon after the war by UNRRA, the U.N., and the American Council on Education developed general patterns and standards, still being followed.

8. Orientation increasingly viewed as continuous process throughout visit.

Advantages claimed include:

1. Gives visitor friendly, informal initial contact with host country.
2. Permits visitor to gain broad understanding of the country, customs, and conditions he will encounter.
3. Places his specialty in perspective by enabling him to relate it to social, economic, and cultural factors.
4. Permits him to check and take steps to strengthen his language facility.
5. Gives him contact with an additional agency or institution, often in a different part of country visited.
6. May help visitor identify and eliminate false stereotypes early in visit.
7. The best programs give experience with the most advanced

educational techniques and with democratic educational practices, i.e., discussion, participant planning, excursions, audio-visual aids.

Factors sometimes overlooked:

1. Tendency to run program like a typical academic course, without adequate adaptation to needs of individuals or particular national groups, or to varying age, special interests, educational background, and language skill.
2. Information-giving likely to be overstressed, at expense of experience.
3. Difficulty in getting participants to adapt quickly to unfamiliar techniques.
4. Sensitive, trained leadership scarce.
5. Participants, unless advised sufficiently in advance, may be impatient at delay in beginning specialized programs, and mistake orientation for effort to propagandize, especially if it precedes government-financed projects.

Research and evaluation:

The agencies pioneering in this approach just after the war— UNRRA and the American Council on Education—stressed evaluation and developed simple standards.

The Institute of International Education—State Department summer programs include evaluation conferences and attempt, through leadership planning and evaluation conferences, the development of common standards. The American Council on Education orientation center includes evaluative discussions in its program, and has conducted a conference on evaluation in June 1952. Shipboard orientation stresses leisurely evaluation on the return trip. Research and evaluation projects now under way through the Social Science Research Council, the Institute of International Education, and the State Department may throw further light upon the value of orientation in international cultural relations.

A *partial list of agencies with operating or coordinating experience:*

AMERICAN ASSOCIATION OF COLLEGES FOR TEACHER EDUCATION

AMERICAN COUNCIL ON EDUCATION, WASHINGTON INTERNATIONAL CENTER

COUNCIL ON STUDENT TRAVEL

DEPARTMENT OF STATE

INSTITUTE OF INTERNATIONAL EDUCATION

NATIONAL SOCIAL WELFARE ASSEMBLY, YOUTH DIVISION

SOCIAL SCIENCE RESEARCH COUNCIL

Numerous institutions having orientation programs for foreign students. These include American University, Washington, D.C.; Haverford College; Columbia University; University of California; Indiana University; Yale University; University of Denver; University of Texas.

HOSPITALITY PROGRAMS

Purposes include:

1. To ensure contact by visitors from abroad with home and family life of host country.
2. To provide personal, individualized assistance in meeting problems of visitors.
3. To provide stimulating and informative contact by nationals of host country with visitors from abroad.
4. To increase likelihood that the visit will result in building of lasting friendships.

Characteristics include:

1. Sponsored by private agencies, usually local.
2. Stresses visits to typical homes under natural circumstances.
3. Usually includes social and cultural events in which host nationals and visitors participate jointly.
4. May include additional services, such as the meeting of new arrivals at boats, planes, and trains, help in shopping, sightseeing, and assistance in making needed contacts.
5. Usually involves contact with community organizations or with international houses or centers.

6. Ideally involves reciprocal relationship enabling visitor to share his special knowledge or talents with his hosts.
7. Usually operated almost entirely by unpaid volunteer workers.

Advantages claimed include:

1. Ensures friendly contact by visitor with individuals, as well as with organized groups and agencies.
2. Gives visitor insight into basic aspects of a culture—its home and community life.
3. Provides a basis for meeting common needs often overlooked in large projects, such as desire to get well acquainted with individuals, need for shopping, interest in sightseeing, etc.
4. Can provide useful insights into visitor's reactions and opinions, including evidences of dissatisfaction, which might not come out in group situations.
5. Under favorable circumstances, may lead to correspondence and lasting personal friendships.
6. Tends to overcome suspicion of ulterior motives, particularly in case of government-financed programs.

Factors sometimes overlooked:

1. Easy to overdo hospitality and "patronize" visitors. "Education" of those concerned is necessary to make it a really valuable experience for both. Hosts and visitors frequently fail to follow through, thus creating bad feeling.
2. Visitors vary in desire and need for hospitality; some prefer privacy and time to themselves.
3. Difficult to conduct naturally, so that visitors are not merely invited for holidays, or as "show-pieces" at dinner parties.
4. Hosts and guests must be carefully matched. Some in each category have a slanted impression of their countries.

Research and evaluation:

As applied to students, the new research projects of the Social Science Research Council and the Institute of International Education may throw light upon how hospitality may relate to other approaches and to satisfying study experiences. Syracuse University, among others, is also studying this problem. The Committee on Friendly Relations Among Foreign Students is constantly making informal studies of its techniques, and conducts an annual census of foreign students in the United States.

A *partial list of agencies with operating or coordinating experience:*

AMERICAN COUNCIL ON EDUCATION, WASHINGTON INTERNATIONAL CENTER

COMMITTEE ON FRIENDLY RELATIONS AMONG FOREIGN STUDENTS

GREATER NEW YORK COUNCIL ON FOREIGN STUDENTS

JUNIOR LEAGUE

INSTITUTE OF INTERNATIONAL EDUCATION

INTERNATIONAL HOUSES *in* Berkeley, Chicago, New York City, Washington, Philadelphia, Boston (Cambridge), and elsewhere

UNITED COUNCIL OF CHURCH WOMEN

APPENDIX

Addresses of Agencies

ADVISORY COMMI᠁ ᴀON ON EDUCATIONAL EXCHANGE
ADVISORY COMMISSION ON INFORMATION
ADVISORY COMMITTEE ON VOLUNTARY FOREIGN AID
  See U.S. Department of State

AFFILIATION OF SCHOOLS AND SEMINARS FOR INTERNATIONAL STUDY AND TRAVEL
545 Fifth Avenue
New York, N.Y.

AMERICAN ASSOCIATION OF COLLEGES FOR TEACHER EDUCATION
State Teachers College
Oneonta, New York

AMERICAN ASSOCIATION OF MUSEUMS
Old National Museum Building
Washington, D.C.

AMERICAN ASSOCIATION OF UNIVERSITY WOMEN
1634 Eye Street N.W.
Washington 6, D.C.

AMERICAN BOOK PUBLISHERS COUNCIL
2 West 46th Street
New York 19, N.Y.

AMERICAN CHEMICAL SOCIETY
1155 Sixteenth Street N.W.
Washington 6, D.C.

AMERICAN COUNCIL OF VOLUNTARY AGENCIES FOR FOREIGN SERVICE
20 West Fortieth Street
New York 18, N.Y.

AMERICAN COUNCIL ON EDUCATION
  Inter-American Schools Service
  Washington International Center
1785 Massachusetts Avenue N.W.
Washington 6, D.C.

AMERICAN DENTAL ASSOCIATION
222 East Superior Street
Chicago 11, Illinois

AMERICAN FARM BUREAU FEDERATION
Munsey Building
Washington, D.C.

AMERICAN FEDERATION OF ARTS
1262 New Hampshire Avenue N.W.
Washington 6, D.C.

AMERICAN FEDERATION OF TEACHERS
28 East Jackson Boulevard
Chicago 4, Illinois

AMERICAN FIELD SERVICE
113 East Thirtieth Street
New York 16, N.Y.

AMERICAN FRIENDS SERVICE COMMITTEE
  Quaker International Voluntary Service
  School Affiliation Service
20 South Twelfth Street
Philadelphia 7, Pennsylvania

AMERICAN HOME ECONOMICS ASSOCIATION
1600 Twentieth Street N.W.
Washington, D.C.

AMERICAN JEWISH JOINT DISTRIBUTION COMMITTEE, INC.
270 Madison Avenue
New York 16, N.Y.

AMERICAN JUNIOR RED CROSS
  See American National Red Cross

AMERICAN LIBRARY ASSOCIATION
  International Relations Office
Library of Congress Annex
Washington 25, D.C.

AMERICAN NATIONAL RED CROSS
  Junior Red Cross
Seventeenth and D Streets N.W.
Washington 13, D.C.

AMERICAN NATIONAL THEATER AND ACADEMY
139 West 44th Street
New York 19, N.Y.

AMERICAN NURSES' ASSOCIATION, INC.
2 Park Avenue
New York 16, N.Y.

AMERICAN RED CROSS
  See American National Red Cross

AMERICAN-SCANDINAVIAN FOUNDATION
116 East 64th Street
New York 31, N.Y.

AMERICAN SYMPHONY ORCHESTRA LEAGUE, INC.
Post Office Box 164
Charleston, West Virginia

AMERICAN TRAVEL ASSOCIATION
1201 Sixteenth Street N.W.
Washington 6, D.C.

AMERICAN YOUTH HOSTELS
6 East 39th Street
New York 16, N.Y.

ASSOCIATION FOR CHILDHOOD EDUCATION
1200 Fifteenth Street N.W.
Washington 5, D.C.

ASSOCIATION OF INTERNATIONAL WORK CAMPS FOR PEACE
110 Avenue Mozart
Paris 16, France

BELGIAN-AMERICAN EDUCATION FOUNDATION, INC.
420 Lexington Avenue
New York 17, N.Y.

BOARD OF FOREIGN SCHOLARSHIPS
  See U.S. Department of State

BOY SCOUTS OF AMERICA
2 Park Avenue
New York 16, N.Y.

BRETHREN SERVICE COMMISSION
22 South State Street
Elgin, Illinois

BRITISH-AMERICAN FOUNDATION FOR EUROPEAN EDUCATION
18 Pine Street
New York 5, N.Y.

BRITISH COUNCIL
65 Davies Street
London W. 1, England

CAMP FIRE GIRLS
88 Lexington Avenue
New York 16, N.Y.

CARE
    CARE Book Plan
20 Broad Street
New York 5, N.Y.

CARL SCHURZ MEMORIAL FOUNDATION, INC.
420 Chestnut Street
Philadelphia 6, Pennsylvania

CARNEGIE CORPORATION OF NEW YORK
522 Fifth Avenue
New York 18, N.Y.

CARNEGIE ENDOWMENT FOR INTERNATIONAL PEACE
405 West 117th Street
New York 27, N.Y.

CARRIE CHAPMAN CATT FOUNDATION
461 Fourth Street
New York 16, N.Y.

CENTRAL DEPARTMENT OF CHURCH WORLD SERVICE
    See National Council of the Churches of Christ in the U.S.A.

CHINA INSTITUTE IN AMERICA
125 East 65th Street
New York 21, N.Y.

CHRISTIAN WORK CAMPS FELLOWSHIP OF CANADA
Box 81
Postal Station D
Toronto, Ontario, Canada

CHURCH WORLD SERVICE
214 East 21st Street
New York, N.Y.

COMMITTEE ON AFRICAN STUDENTS IN NORTH AMERICA
166 Fifth Avenue
New York 10, N.Y.

COMMITTEE ON FRIENDLY RELATIONS AMONG FOREIGN STUDENTS
347 Madison Avenue
New York 17, N.Y.

COMMITTEE ON INTERNATIONAL EXCHANGE OF PERSONS
    See Conference Board of Associated Research Councils

COMMITTEE ON INTERNATIONAL SCIENTIFIC PUBLICATIONS
    See National Research Council

COMMITTEE ON VOLUNTARY INTERNATIONAL ASSISTANCE
    See U.S. National Commission for UNESCO

COMMONWEALTH FUND
41 East 57th Street
New York, N.Y.

CONFERENCE BOARD OF ASSOCIATED RESEARCH COUNCILS
    Committee on International Exchange of Persons
2101 Constitution Avenue
Washington 25, D.C.

CONGREGATIONAL CHRISTIAN SERVICE COMMISSION
110 East 29th Street
New York 16, N.Y.

COORDINATING COMMITTEE FOR INTERNATIONAL WORK CAMPS
c/o Education Department, UNESCO
19 Avenue Kléber
Paris 16e, France

COUNCIL ON STUDENT TRAVEL
156 Fifth Avenue
New York 17, N.Y.

DARIEN BOOK AID PLAN
Darien, Connecticut

DEPARTMENT OF AGRICULTURE
See U.S. Department of Agriculture

DEPARTMENT OF THE ARMY
See U.S. Department of the Army

DEPARTMENT OF STATE
See U.S. Department of State

EDUCATIONAL EXCHANGE SERVICE, INTERNATIONAL INFORMATION ADMINISTRATION
See U.S. Department of State

ENGLISH-SPEAKING UNION
Pen Friends Division
19 East 54th Street
New York 22, N.Y.

EXPERIMENT IN INTERNATIONAL LIVING
Putney, Vermont

FÉDÉRATION INTERNATIONALE DES ORGANISATIONS DE CORRESPONDANCE ET D'ECHANGES SCOLAIRES (FIOCES)
29 rue d'Ulm
Paris V, France

THE FORD FOUNDATION
655 Madison Avenue
New York 21, N.Y.

FULBRIGHT ACT
Graduate students
Fulbright Division, Institute of International Education
857 Fifth Avenue
New York 21, N.Y.
Professors, specialists, and advanced research scholars
Conference Board of Associated Research Councils
2101 Constitution Avenue
Washington 25, D.C.
Teachers in American schools abroad
American Council on Education
1785 Massachusetts Avenue N.W.
Washington 6, D.C.

FULBRIGHT ACT—*Continued*
  Teachers in national schools abroad
    U.S. Office of Education
    Federal Security Agency
    Washington 25, D.C.

GENERAL FEDERATION OF WOMEN'S CLUBS
1734 N Street N.W.
Washington, D.C.

GIRL SCOUTS OF AMERICA
155 East 44th Street
New York 17, N.Y.

GOVERNMENTAL AFFAIRS INSTITUTE, INC.
1785 Massachusetts Avenue N.W.
Washington 6, D.C.

GREATER NEW YORK COUNCIL OF FOREIGN STUDENTS
500 Riverside Drive
New York 27, N.Y.

GREEK WAR RELIEF ASSOCIATION, INC., U.S.A.
221 West 57th Street
New York 19, N.Y.

GUGGENHEIM FOUNDATION (JOHN SIMON GUGGENHEIM MEMORIAL
  FOUNDATION)
551 Fifth Avenue
New York 17, N.Y.

HARRIS FOUNDATION OF ROTARY INTERNATIONAL
Rotary International
35 East Wacker Drive
Chicago, Illinois

HARVARD UNIVERSITY
  Department of Social Relations
Cambridge, Massachusetts

EDWARD W. HAZEN FOUNDATION
400 Prospect Street
New Haven 11, Connecticut

INSTITUTE FOR RESEARCH IN HUMAN RELATIONS
2224 Locust Street
Philadelphia, Pennsylvania

INSTITUTE OF INTERNATIONAL EDUCATION
1 East 67th Street
New York 21, N.Y.

INTER-AMERICAN SCHOOLS SERVICE
American Council on Education
1785 Massachusetts Avenue N.W.
Washington 6, D.C.

INTERNATIONAL BASIC ECONOMY CORPORATION
30 Rockefeller Plaza
New York, N.Y.

INTERNATIONAL COUNCIL OF NURSES
    See American Nurses' Association, Inc.

INTERNATIONAL FARM YOUTH EXCHANGE
National 4-H Club Foundation
c/o Extension Service
U.S. Department of Agriculture
Washington 25, D.C.

INTERNATIONAL FEDERATION OF AGRICULTURAL PRODUCERS
712 Jackson Place N.W.
Washington, D.C.

INTERNATIONAL FEDERATION OF UNIVERSITY WOMEN
    See American Association of University Women

INTERNATIONAL FRIENDSHIP LEAGUE
40 Mount Vernon Street
Boston 8, Massachusetts

INTERNATIONAL HOUSE ALUMNI ASSOCIATION
500 Riverside Drive
New York, N.Y.

INTERNATIONAL HOUSES
    University of California, Berkeley 4, California
    500 Riverside Drive, New York, N.Y.
    1414 East 59th Street, Chicago 37, Illinois
    33 Garden Street, Cambridge 38, Massachusetts
    3905 Spruce Street, Philadelphia 4, Pennsylvania
    1825 R Street N.W., Washington 9, D.C.

INTERNATIONAL INFORMATION ADMINISTRATION
    See U.S. Department of State

INTERNATIONAL LABOR OFFICE
Palais des Nations
Geneva, Switzerland

INTERNATIONAL STUDENTS SOCIETY
Hillsboro, Oregon

INTERNATIONAL WORK STUDENT EXCHANGE
   (Inactive at present)

INTERNATIONAL YOUTH HOSTELS FEDERATION
   See American Youth Hostels

JAPANESE INTERNATIONAL CHRISTIAN UNIVERSITY FOUNDATION, INC.
123 College Place
Syracuse, New York

JUNIOR LEAGUE (ASSOCIATION OF THE JUNIOR LEAGUES OF AMERICA, INC.)
The Waldorf-Astoria
New York 22, N.Y.

JUNIOR RED CROSS
   See American National Red Cross

W. K. KELLOGG FOUNDATION
250 Champion Street
Battle Creek, Michigan

LEAGUE OF WOMEN VOTERS
726 Jackson Place N.W.
Washington 6, D.C.

LIBRARY OF CONGRESS
Washington 25, D.C.

LISLE FELLOWSHIP, INC.
20 West Fortieth Street
New York 18, N.Y.

LOUIS AUGUST JONAS FOUNDATION, INC.
Post Office Drawer No. 33
Walden, New York

MASSACHUSETTS INSTITUTE OF TECHNOLOGY
   International Student Project
Cambridge 39, Massachusetts

MEDWAY PLAN
Woodbury, Connecticut

MENNONITE CENTRAL COMMITTEE, INC.
  Mennonite Voluntary Service
Akron, Pennsylvania

METHODIST STUDENT SERVICE
  Methodist Youth Fellowship
c/o Rev. R. C. Singleton
150 Fifth Avenue
New York 11, N.Y.

MUSIC EDUCATORS NATIONAL CONFERENCE
  See National Education Association

MUTUAL SECURITY AGENCY
Washington 25, D.C.

NATIONAL ART EDUCATION ASSOCIATION
  See National Education Association

NATIONAL ARTS FOUNDATION
60 Broadway
New York, N.Y.

NATIONAL ASSOCIATION OF FOREIGN STUDENT ADVISERS
2 West 45th Street
New York 19, N.Y.

NATIONAL BUREAU OF EDUCATIONAL CORRESPONDENCE
George Peabody College for Teachers
Nashville 4, Tennessee

NATIONAL CATHOLIC EDUCATIONAL ASSOCIATION
1785 Massachusetts Avenue N.W.
Washington 6, D.C.

NATIONAL CATHOLIC WELFARE CONFERENCE
1312 Massachusetts Avenue N.W.
Washington 5, D.C.

NATIONAL CIO COMMUNITY SERVICE COMMITTEE
1776 Broadway
New York, N.Y.

NATIONAL COMMISSION FOR UNESCO
   See U.S. National Commission for UNESCO

NATIONAL CONFERENCE OF CHRISTIANS AND JEWS
381 Fourth Avenue
New York 16, N.Y.

NATIONAL CONGRESS OF PARENTS AND TEACHERS
600 South Michigan Boulevard
Chicago 5, Illinois

NATIONAL COUNCIL OF THE CHURCHES OF CHRIST IN THE U.S.A.
   Central Department of Church World Service
122 Maryland Avenue N.E.
Washington, D.C.

NATIONAL COUNCIL OF FARMER COOPERATIVES
744 Jackson Place
Washington 6, D.C.

NATIONAL COUNCIL OF JEWISH WOMEN
1819 Broadway
New York 23, N.Y.

NATIONAL EDUCATION ASSOCIATION OF THE UNITED STATES
   Committee on International Relations
      United Nations Educational Service
   Division of Travel Service
   Music Educators National Conference
   National Art Education Association
   World Organization of the Teaching Profession
1201 Sixteenth Street N.W.
Washington 6, D.C.

NATIONAL RESEARCH COUNCIL
   Committee on International Scientific Publications
28 Newbury Street
Boston 16, Massachusetts

NATIONAL SOCIAL WELFARE ASSEMBLY
   Youth Division
134 East 56th Street
New York 22, N.Y.

NATIONAL STUDENT ASSOCIATION
96 Winthrop Street
Cambridge 38, Massachusetts

NATIONAL TRAINING LABORATORY IN GROUP RELATIONS
Bethel, Maine

NEAR EAST COLLEGE ASSOCIATION
46 Cedar Street
New York 5, N.Y.

NEAR EAST FOUNDATION
54 East 64th Street
New York 21, N.Y.

NEW YORK HERALD TRIBUNE HIGH SCHOOL FORUM
New York Herald Tribune
230 West 41st Street
New York 18, N.Y.

OFFICE OF FOREIGN AGRICULTURAL RELATIONS
  See U.S. Department of Agriculture

OPERATION DEMOCRACY, INC.
369 Lexington Avenue
New York 17, N.Y.

PEN FRIENDS DIVISION
  See English-Speaking Union

QUAKER INTERNATIONAL VOLUNTARY SERVICE
  See American Friends Service Committee

RHODES SCHOLARSHIP TRUST
American Selection Committee
Institute for Advanced Study
Princeton, New Jersey

ROCKEFELLER FOUNDATION
49 West 49th Street
New York 20, N.Y.

ROTARY INTERNATIONAL
  Harris Foundation of Rotary International
35 East Wacker Drive
Chicago 1, Illinois

SALZBURG SEMINAR IN AMERICAN STUDIES
Phillips Brooks House
Cambridge 38, Massachusetts

SAVE THE CHILDREN FEDERATION, INC.
1 Madison Avenue
New York 10, N.Y.

SCHOOL AFFILIATION SERVICE
    See American Friends Service Committee

SERVICE CIVIL INTERNATIONAL
77 Boulevard Jean Jaurés
Clichy, Seine, France

SMITHSONIAN INSTITUTION
    International Exchange Service
Washington 25, D.C.

SOCIAL SCIENCE RESEARCH COUNCIL
230 Park Avenue
New York 17, N.Y.

STUDENT FORUM ON INTERNATIONAL RELATIONS
Post Office Box 733
San Francisco, California

STUDENT LETTER EXCHANGE
Waseca, Minnesota

TECHNICAL ASSISTANCE ADMINISTRATION
United Nations
New York

TECHNICAL COOPERATION ADMINISTRATION
    See U.S. Department of State

TOWN MEETING OF THE AIR
123 West 43rd Street
New York, N.Y.

UNESCO [United Nations Educational, Scientific and Cultural Organization]
    19 Avenue Kléber
Paris 16ᵉ, France

UNESCO RELATIONS STAFF
  See U.S. Department of State

UNESCO, U.S. NATIONAL COMMISSION FOR
  See U.S. National Commission for UNESCO

UNESCO VOLUNTARY INTERNATIONAL ASSISTANCE (Unesco Gift Coupon Plan)
United Nations Building
New York, N.Y.

UNION OF INTERNATIONAL ASSOCIATIONS
Palais d'Egmont
Brussels, Belgium

UNITARIAN SERVICE COMMITTEE, INC.
9 Park Street
Boston 8, Massachusetts

UNITED CHRISTIAN YOUTH MOVEMENT, YOUTH SERVICE PROJECTS, U.S.A.
79 East Adams Street
Chicago 3, Illinois

UNITED COUNCIL OF CHURCH WOMEN
156 Fifth Avenue
New York 10, N.Y.

UNITED NATIONS
New York, N.Y.

UNITED STATES BOOK EXCHANGE, INC.
Library of Congress
Washington 25, D.C.

UNIVERSALIST SERVICE COMMITTEE
16 Beacon Street
Boston 8, Massachusetts

UNIVERSITY OF MICHIGAN
  Group Relations Laboratory
Ann Arbor, Michigan

U.S. DEPARTMENT OF AGRICULTURE
  International Farm Youth Exchange, National 4-H Club
    Foundation
  Office of Foreign Agricultural Relations
Washington 25, D.C.

U.S. DEPARTMENT OF THE ARMY
  HICOG (U.S. High Commissioner for Germany)
Pentagon
Arlington, Virginia

U.S. DEPARTMENT OF STATE
  Advisory Commission on Educational Exchange
  Advisory Commission on Information
  Advisory Committee on Voluntary Foreign Aid
  Board of Foreign Scholarships
  Educational Exchange Service of the International Information Ad-
    ministration
  Technical Cooperation Administration
  UNESCO Relations Staff
  U.S. National Commission for UNESCO
Washington 25, D.C.

U.S. NATIONAL COMMISSION FOR UNESCO
  Committee on Voluntary International Assistance
c/o Department of State
Washington 25, D.C.

U.S. OFFICE OF EDUCATION
Federal Security Agency
Washington 25, D.C.

WALDORF SCHOOLS FUND, INC.
15 East 79th Street
New York 21, N.Y.

WASHINGTON INTERNATIONAL CENTER
American Council on Education
1785 Massachusetts Avenue N.W.
Washington 6, D.C.

WOMEN'S INTERNATIONAL LEAGUE FOR PEACE AND FREEDOM
2006 Walnut Street
Philadelphia 3, Pennsylvania

WOODROW WILSON SCHOOL OF PUBLIC AND INTERNATIONAL AFFAIRS
Princeton University
Princeton, New Jersey

WORLD ALLIANCE OF YMCA's
  See Young Men's Christian Association

WORLD BROTHERHOOD
65 Quai d'Orsay
Paris, France
or
c/o National Conference of Christians and Jews
381 Fourth Avenue
New York 16, N.Y.

WORLD COUNCIL OF CHURCHES
156 Fifth Avenue
New York, N.Y.

WORLD FEDERATION FOR MENTAL HEALTH
19 Manchester Street
London W. 1, England

WORLD ORGANIZATION OF THE TEACHING PROFESSION
See National Educational Association

WORLD STUDENT SERVICE FUND
20 West 40th Street
New York 18, N.Y.

WORLD UNION OF JEWISH STUDENTS
(Address unknown)

WORLD UNIVERSITY SERVICE
13 rue Calvin
Geneva, Switzerland

YOUNG MEN'S CHRISTIAN ASSOCIATION, NATIONAL COUNCIL OF
291 Broadway
New York 7, N.Y.

YOUNG WOMEN'S CHRISTIAN ASSOCIATION OF THE UNITED STATES OF
AMERICA
600 Lexington Avenue
New York 22, N.Y.

YOUTH OF ALL NATIONS, INC.
16 St. Luke's Place
New York 14, N.Y.

YOUTH ARGOSY, INC.
Northfield, Massachusetts

Bibliography

Adorno, T. W.; Frenkel-Brunswik, E.; Levinson, D. J.; and Sanford, H. N. *The Authoritarian Personality*. New York: Harper & Bros., 1950. 990 pp.

Adams, Thomas R. *Education for International Understanding*. New York: Institute of Adult Education, 1948. 181 pp.

Arndt, Christian O., and Everett, Samuel. *Education for a World Society*. New York: Harper & Bros., 1951. 263 pp.

Bigelow, Karl W. (ed.). *Cultural Groups and Human Relations*. New York: Bureau of Publications, Teachers College, Columbia University, 1951. 214 pp.

Brogan, D. W. *The American Character*. New York: Knopf Co., 1944. 169 pp.

Bryson, Lyman (ed.). *Approaches to Group Understanding*. New York: Harper & Bros., 1947. 858 pp.

Cantril, Hadley. *The "Why" of Man's Experience*. New York: Macmillan Co., 1950. 177 pp.

——— (ed.). *Tensions That Cause War*. UNESCO Conference Study. Urbana: University of Illinois Press, 1950. 303 pp.

Chase, Stuart. *Roads to Agreement: Successful Methods in the Science of Human Relations*. New York: Harper & Bros., 1951. 240 pp.

Cohen, J. *Human Nature, War and Society*. London: Watts, 1946. 193 pp.

Commager, Henry S. (ed.). *America in Perspective: The United States Through Foreign Eyes*. New York: Random House, 1947. 416 pp.

Dunn, Frederick S. *War and the Minds of Men*. New York: Harper & Bros., and Council on Foreign Relations, 1950. 111 pp.

European Beliefs Regarding the United States. New York: Common Council for American Unity, 1949. 134 pp.

Education for Mutual Understanding and Friendship Between Canada and the United States. Washington: American Council on Education, 1945. 16 pp.

GORER, GOEFFREY. *The American People: A Study in National Character.* New York: W. W. Norton & Co., 1948. 246 pp.

HARRISON, JOSEPH B. (ed.). *If Men Want Peace: The Mandates of World Order.* New York: Macmillan Co., 1946. 292 pp.

HEINDEL, RICHARD H. *The American Impact on Great Britain, 1898–1914.* Philadelphia: University of Pennsylvania Press, 1940. 439 pp.

JONES, HOWARD MUMFORD. *Education and World Tragedy.* Cambridge, Mass.: Harvard University Press, 1946. 178 pp.

KANDEL, I. L. *United States Activities in International Cultural Relations.* Washington: American Council on Education, 1945. 102 pp.

KENWORTHY, LEONARD S. *World Horizons for Teachers.* New York: Columbia University Press, 1952. 138 pp.

KISKER, GEORGE W. (ed.). *World Tension: The Psychopathology of International Relations.* New York: Prentice-Hall, Inc., 1951. 317 pp.

KLINEBERG, OTTO. *Tensions Affecting International Understanding: A Survey of Research.* New York: Social Science Research Council, 1950. 217 pp.

KLUCKHOHN, CLYDE. "An Anthropologist Looks at the United States," *Mirror for Man.* New York: McGraw-Hill Book Co., 1949. 313 pp.

LEIGHTON, ALEXANDER H. *Human Relations in a Changing World: Observations on the Use of the Social Sciences.* New York: E. P. Dutton Co., 1949. 340 pp.

———. *The Governing of Men.* Princeton, N.J.: Princeton University Press, 1945. 397 pp.

LEWIN, KURT. *Resolving Social Conflicts.* New York: Harper & Bros., 1948. 230 pp.

LINTON, RALPH (ed.). *The Science of Man in the World Crisis.* New York: Columbia University Press, 1945. 532 pp.

McCLURE, DOROTHY. *The Treatment of International Agencies in School History Textbooks in the United States.* Washington: Government Printing Office, 1950. 108 pp.

McMURRY, RUTH, and LEE, MUNA. *The Cultural Approach: Another Way in International Relations.* Chapel Hill: University of North Carolina Press, 1947.

MURPHY, GARDNER. *Human Nature and Enduring Peace.* Boston: Houghton Mifflin Co., 1941. 475 pp.

NEVINS, ALLAN (ed.). *America Through British Eyes*. New York: Oxford University Press, 1948. 530 pp.

NOSTRAND, HOWARD LEE, and BROWN, FRANCIS J. *The Role of Colleges and Universities in International Understanding*. Washington: American Council on Education, 1949. 137 pp.

PEAR, T. H. (ed.). *Psychological Factors of Peace and War*. New York: Philosophical Library, 1950. 255 pp.

QUILLEN, I. JAMES. *Textbook Improvement and International Understanding*. Washington: American Council on Education, 1948. 78 pp.

ROOSEVELT, ELEANOR, and FERRIS, HELEN. *Partners: The United Nations and Youth*. Garden City: Doubleday & Co., 1950. 200 pp.

ROSENHAUPT, HANS W. *How to Wage Peace*. New York: John Day Co., 1949. 248 pp.

RUSSELL SAGE FOUNDATION. *Effective Use of Social Science Research in the Federal Services*. New York: The Foundation, 1950. 47 pp.

U.S. DEPARTMENT OF STATE. "External Research Report." Mimeographed. Washington: The Department. Issued at frequent intervals.

———. *Field Reporter*. Washington: The Department. Bimonthly.

VANDERSCHMIDT, FRED. *What the English Think of Us*. New York: McBride Co., 1948. 212 pp.

VISSON, ANDRÉ. *As Others See Us*. New York: Doubleday & Co., 1948. 252 pp.

WALSH, EDMUND A. *Total Empire: The Roots and Progress of World Communism*. Milwaukee: Bruce Publishing Co., 1951.

WILSON, HOWARD E. *Universities and World Affairs*. New York: Carnegie Endowment for International Peace, 1951. 88 pp.

CIER AND COA PUBLICATIONS

AUSTIN, MARGRETTA S. *It's Yours for the Giving*. Paris, UNESCO; Washington, D.C., Commission for International Educational Reconstruction, 1949. 25 pp.

The Bulletin of the Commission for International Educational Reconstruction. Monthly, October 1946–March 1949. Washington, D.C.

KENWORTHY, LEONARD S. *Going to School in War Devastated Countries*. Paris, UNESCO; Washington, D.C., Commission for International Educational Reconstruction, 1947. 18 pp.

Occupied Areas Handbook. A Directory of American Nongovernmental Organizations Engaged in Cultural and Educational Relations with the Occupied Countries. First edition December 1949; second edition May 1950. Washington, D.C.: American Council on Education. 74 pp.

Occupied Countries News Notes. Issues 1–45, 1949–50; semimonthly. Washington, D.C.: Advisory Committee on Cultural and Educational Relations with the Occupied Countries, American Council on Education. Mimeographed.

SNYDER, HAROLD E., and AUSTIN, MARGRETTA S. (eds.). *Cultural Relations with the Occupied Countries.* A Report of the First National Conference on the Occupied Countries Held under the Auspices of the Commission on the Occupied Areas of the American Council on Education in Cooperation with the Department of State, Washington, D.C., December 9–10, 1949. Washington, D.C.: American Council on Education, 1950. 107 pp.

——, and AUSTIN, MARGRETTA S. (eds.). *Educational Progress in Japan and the Ryukyus.* A Report of a Conference of Major American Nongovernmental Agencies, Sponsored by the Commission on the Occupied Areas of the American Council on Education with the Cooperation of the Department of the Army, Washington, D.C., May 25, 1950. Washington, D.C.: American Council on Education, 1950. 52 pp.

——, and BEAUCHAMP, GEORGE E. *An Experiment in International Cultural Relations.* A Report of the Staff of the Commission on the Occupied Areas. Washington, D.C.: American Council on Education, 1951. 112 pp.

——, and BEAUCHAMP, GEORGE E. (eds.). *Responsibilities of Voluntary Agencies in Occupied Areas.* A Report of the Second National Conference on the Occupied Countries Held under the Auspices of the Commission on the Occupied Areas of the American Council on Education in Cooperation with the Department of State and the Department of the Army, Washington, D.C., November 30–December 1, 1950. Washington, D.C.: American Council on Education, 1951. 125 pp.

UNESCO PUBLICATIONS

Building Roads to Peace: Exchange of People Between the United States and Other Countries. Paris: United Nations Educational, Scientific and Cultural Organization.

A Handbook for the Improvement of Textbooks and Teaching Materials as Aids to International Understanding. Paris, 1949. 172 pp.

Handbook on the International Exchange of Publications. Paris.

International Social Science Bulletin. Quarterly. Paris.

KENWORTHY, LEONARD S. *The Teacher and the Post-War Child in War Devastated Countries*. Paris, 1946. 48 pp.

Reports of Educational Missions. Paris.

Study Abroad. International Handbook of Fellowships, Scholarships, Educational Exchange. Vol. I, 1948. Vol. III, 1950–51. New York: Columbia University Press, 1951. 307 pp.

U.S. NATIONAL COMMISSION FOR UNESCO

Newsletter. Washington, D.C.: Department of State. Biweekly.

The Unesco Story. Washington, D.C.: Department of State, 1950. 112 pp.

Various pamphlets describing the UNESCO Gift Coupon Plan and other cultural relations programs.

Index

Action approaches, international cultural relations, 97–177
Advisory Committee on Voluntary Foreign Aid of U.S. Department of State, 59, 65, 129, 132, 141, 142, 148, 149, 150, 178, 192
Affiliation of Schools and Seminars for International Travel and Study, 138, 178
Affiliations, 151–63
  advantages, 152
  of colleges and universities, 157–59
  of communities, 160–63
  limitations, 152
  of organizations, 153–54
  of schools, 155–57
Allport, Gordon W., 17, 18, 107, 120
American Anthropological Society, 18
American Association of Colleges for Teacher Education, 53, 159, 175, 178
American Association of Junior Colleges, 51
American Association of Museums, 171, 178
American Association of School Administrators, 64
American Association of University Women, 49, 53, 102, 112, 113, 178
American Book Publishers Council, 145, 178
American Chemical Society, 113, 178
American Council on Education, v, 39, 40, 41, 42, 51, 54, 64, 65, 67–70, 72, 87, 95, 115, 135, 153, 159, 173, 174, 179
  Inter-American Schools Service, 27, 110, 169, 179, 185
  Washington International Center, 135, 174, 175, 177, 179
American Council of Learned Societies, 21
American Council of Voluntary Agencies for Foreign Service, 59, 115, 132, 141, 142, 145, 147, 148, 149, 150, 153, 178

American Dental Association, 129, 148, 179
American Farm Bureau Federation, 107, 179
American Federation of Arts, 171, 179
American Federation of Teachers, 64, 110, 148, 179
American Field Service, 104–5, 179
American Friends Service Committee, v, 14–15, 105, 115, 117, 118, 120, 121, 124, 132, 135, 147, 148, 150, 152, 156, 157, 179
  Washington Seminar, v, 14–15
American Home Economics Association, 113, 179
American Jewish Joint Distribution Committee, Inc., 49, 145, 179
American Junior Red Cross, 105, 150, 165, 179
American Library Association, 53, 141, 144, 145, 179
American National Red Cross, 49, 52, 53, 113, 124, 147, 148, 172, 180
American National Theater and Academy, 172, 180
American Nurses Association, 180
American Psychological Association, 18
American-Scandinavian Foundation, Inc., 113, 180
American-supported institutions abroad, 167–70
American Symphony Orchestra League, Inc., 172, 180
American Travel Association, Inc., 138, 180
American University, 175
American Youth Hostels, 108, 180
Angell, Robert C., 16
Arden House, 15
Association of American Universities, 71
Association for Childhood Education, 53, 148, 180
Association of International Workcamps for Peace, 120, 121, 180
Austin, Margretta S., 52

199

humanities, 18–22
interdisciplinary studies, 13, 15
social science contributions, 10–18
tensions, 16
values, as factors in, 18–22, 45–46, 82–84
International Service Centers (proposed), 71–72
International student houses, 135, 177, 185
International Students Society, 167, 186
International Work Student Exchange (inactive at present), 108, 186
International Youth Hostels Federation, 121, 186. *See also* American Youth Hostels Federation

Japanese International Christian University Foundation, Inc., 169, 186
Jonas Foundation, Inc. *See* Louis August Jonas Foundation, Inc.
Junior League (Association of the Junior Leagues of America, Inc.), 177, 186
Junior Red Cross. *See* American Junior Red Cross

Kandel, I. L., 24–25
Kellogg Foundation. *See* W. K. Kellogg Foundation
Kenworthy, Leonard, 35 fn., 48, 52
Kisker, George W., 16
Klineberg, Otto, 16
Koo, Ambassador V. K. Wellington, 56

League of Women Voters, 113, 186
Lee Journalism Foundation of Washington and Lee University, 112
Lee, Muna, 23, 24, 25
Leighton, Alexander H., 17, 19
Leland, Waldo G., 56
Library of Congress, 29, 141, 145, 186
Likert, Rensis, 18
Lisle Fellowship, Inc., 124, 165, 186
Louis August Jonas Foundation, Inc., 108, 186

McClelland, David, 21
McCormick, Charles G., 124

McCormick, Mary Jane, 124
MacLeish, Archibald, 23
McMurry, R. E., 23, 24, 25
Margue, N., 57
Marshall Plan. *See* Economic Cooperation Administration
Maryland, University of, 53
Massachusetts Institute of Technology International Student Project, 117, 118, 186
Massachusetts State College, 124
Materials, interchange of, 139–50
advantages, 139–40
educational, 140–42, 145–48
limitations, 140
publications, 140–41, 142–45
relief supplies, 148–50
Medway Plan, 162, 187
Mennonite Central Committee, Inc., 108, 187
Mennonite Voluntary Service, 121, 187
Methodist Student Service, 121, 187
Michigan State College, 159
Michigan, University of, Group Relations Laboratory, 125, 191
Music Educators National Conference of the National Education Association, 172, 188
Mutual Security Agency, 29, 30, 129, 132, 187

National Art Education Association of the National Education Association, 172, 188
National Arts Foundation, 172, 187
National Association of Foreign Student Advisers, 66, 102, 103, 187
National Association of Secondary-School Principals, 51
National Bureau of Educational Correspondence, 167, 187
National Catholic Educational Association, 113, 150, 159, 187
National Catholic Welfare Conference, 49, 105, 142, 148, 187
National CIO Community Service Committee, 103, 187
National Commission for UNESCO. *See* U.S. National Commission for UNESCO

AMERICAN COUNCIL ON EDUCATION

ARTHUR S. ADAMS, *President*

The American Council on Education is a *council* of national educational associations; organizations having related interests; approved universities, colleges, teachers colleges, junior colleges, technological schools, and selected private secondary schools; state departments of education; city school systems and private school systems; selected educational departments of business and industrial companies; voluntary associations of higher education in the states; and large public libraries. It is a center of cooperation and coordination whose influence has been apparent in the shaping of American educational policies and the formulation of educational practices during the last thirty-four years.